MW00637194

Praise for *Everything Could Be a Prayer*

"I love everything about this book—the art, the guidance for practicing *visio divina*, the spiritual depth of the meditations, and the chosen subjects of those meditations. Kreg Yingst has generously contributed his artistry to our ministry here in the Transforming Center, and we have all been stunned by its beauty and depth. His gifts have blessed us profoundly, and now, through this book, his ministry will be made even more widely accessible. What a gift!"

—**Ruth Haley Barton**, founder of the Transforming Center and author of *Sacred Rhythms*

"As bold and beautiful as any brightly painted Book of Hours, *Everything Could Be a Prayer* is the most exuberant, vibrant reimagining of *visio divina* yet. Kreg Yingst has made a portal for meditating with Howard Thurman, Black Elk, Fannie Lou Hamer, Brother Lawrence, Amma Theodora, Abba Moses, Dorothy Day, Teresa of Ávila, Clare of Assisi, Thomas Merton, and many other mystics and justice-seekers. Its abundant love will rock your heart!"

—**Carmen Acevedo Butcher**, PhD, poet and translator of Brother Lawrence's *Practice of the Presence* and *The Cloud of Unknowing*

"I've been a huge fan of the art of Kreg Yingst for many years. His printmaking inspires and challenges me in my artmaking in all of the best ways. And in addition to a common love of materials, we seem to share a love for many of the same saints. It feels like all of my favorites are here—Brendan, Corrie ten Boom, Nicholas of Myra, Sojourner Truth, Patrick, Albrecht Durer, Hildegard of Bingen, C. S. Lewis—and so many more. This is a wonderful book. My only problem with it is that he made it before I got to!"

—**Ned Bustard**, printmaker and designer of *Every Moment Holy*

"Beauty! Biography! Prayer! *Everything Could Be a Prayer* is the perfect intersection for nourishment in these challenging times. My spirits were raised and my heart expanded reading and pondering each page. This book is manna in these desert times."

—**Simone Campbell**, SSS, author of *A Nun on the Bus* and *Hunger for Hope*, and recipient of the 2022 Presidential Medal of Freedom

"I have never experienced a book quite like *Everything Could Be a Prayer*, and I use the word 'experience' intentionally. What Kreg Yingst offers us in this book goes far beyond words and images on a page; it is an invitation to be enveloped in the mystery of Divine Love. I found my heart moved with such joy as I was brought into conversation with so many saints and mystics from across the expanse of time and tradition. Sit with this book long enough and you will begin to see with new eyes, which is just what the mystics hoped and prayed for."

—**Drew Jackson**, poet and author of *God Speaks Through Wombs* and *Touch the Earth*

"Bold Dorothy Day dismissed 'blind and power-loving and greedy' Christians, saying, 'I never expected leadership from them.' Instead, she points us to those Jesus-followers of mercy, goodness, and sacrifice: 'the saints that keep appearing all through history who keep things going.' Through insightfully curated word and stunning art, Kreg Yingst brings us into the company of those luminous ones who keep things going—inviting us, too, to join in the way of redeeming faithfulness."

—**Karen Wright Marsh**, director of Theological Horizons and author of *Vintage Saints and Sinners* and *Wake Up to Wonder*

"Full disclosure: I've been a fan of Kreg Yingst's distinctive and prayerful woodcuts for a number of years now—and I'm delighted to say this new book of his shows that he is as gifted a writer as he is an artist. *Everything Could Be a Prayer* pairs truly insightful introductions to a wide variety of saints, mystics, and holy troublemakers with art that invites you into meditation and contemplation. This book works both as a daily devotional and as a catalog for discovering some truly amazing spiritual exemplars. You'll make some new friends by reading this book—I certainly did."

—**Carl McColman**, author of *The New Big Book of Christian Mysticism* and *Eternal Heart*

"Kreg Yingst is an artist of great craft and soulfulness. His images are windows into the holy. This book of reflections is such a gift. The sheer breadth of mystics included is marvelous. The written invitations to companion his icons are a call to sit and be with the wisdom offered and let them transform you. Highly recommended!"

—**Christine Valters Paintner,** online abbess at Abbey of the Arts and author of *A Different Kind of Fast* and other books

"*Everything Could Be a Prayer* is a gem of a book. Kreg Yingst's block prints of mystics, saints, and justice-seekers are inspirational, bringing them to life in a way that provides a wonderful focus for *visio divina*, or sacred seeing. His reflections on the lives of these precious people draw us into the presence of God in beautiful ways. This is a must-read book for all followers of Christ."

—**Christine Sine**, author of *The Gift of Wonder: Creative Practices for Delighting in God*

EVERYTHING COULD BE A PRAYER

EVERYTHING COULD BE A PRAYER

ONE HUNDRED PORTRAITS OF SAINTS AND MYSTICS

Kreg Yingst

Broadleaf Books
Minneapolis

EVERYTHING COULD BE A PRAYER
One Hundred Portraits of Saints and Mystics

Find more of Kreg Yingst's work at https://www.kregyingst.com/.

29 28 27 26 25 24 1 2 3 4 5 6 7 8 9

Library of Congress Control Number: 2023952462 (print)

Cover image: © 2023 Getty Images; Yellow page of the old book on white background/ 506760210 by ZaharovEvgeniy
Cover design: 1517 Media

Print ISBN: 978-1-5064-9948-2
eBook ISBN: 978-1-5064-9949-9

Printed in China.

For my grandchildren—
the next generation of saints and mystics.

Contents

Introduction

I began creating icon-style portraits as a New Year's resolution at the beginning of 2013. Creating them was a means of confronting the darkness around us—more specifically, as a direct response to the Sandy Hook school shooting. Through my art, I wanted to bring light and healing: Something tangible that could be seen and held. Prayers that the viewer could speak. Images to contemplate that might offer a sense of peace and solace.

My daily devotional routine was to find a prayer—one per week—and then meditate on it, draw it, carve it, print it, and paint it. Each block print featured the saint or mystic who had spoken the prayer. By the end of the year, I had completed fifty-two prints.

In the ensuing years, I'd occasionally do one, but my work on these portraits was sporadic at best. Then in 2020 the pandemic struck, and many of us encountered solitude in a new way. George Floyd was murdered by police, and the country and the world faced a renewed reckoning with the persistence of injustice and racism. In despair and dogged by a sense of hopelessness, I decided to again focus on this spiritual discipline. I needed models of faithful Christian witness in times of suffering and fear. This time I searched for the wisdom of self-imposed hermits and leaders from marginalized communities.

The collection that emerged features portraits of people of faith: saints and mystics from different periods, cultures, ethnicities, genders, and denominations. They are contemplatives and activists, well-known and obscure, Orthodox and Protestant and Catholic. Some are monks and nuns and founders of monastic movements, such as Benedict of Nursia, Francis and Clare of Assisi, and St. Ignatius of Loyola. Some are hermits: St. Antony, Abba Poemen, and Amma Syncletica. Some are activists like Óscar Romero, Martin Luther King Jr., and Dorothy Day. Others are creative writers, poets, and artists: Mechthild of Magdeburg, Christina Rossetti, and Albrecht Dürer. Their commonality is their love for God and their enduring awareness of God's love for them.

The saints and mystics in this book share a deep and abiding devotion to Christ, whose essence shines through them. But not all aspects of their lives are commendable. Like the people the writer of Hebrews names as ancients commended for their faith, they were certainly not perfect. Yet put together, these saints and mystics offer us a colorful light spectrum seen through a God-shaped prism, each an individual piece of glass. When the pieces are assembled, they form a stained-glass window that reveals the *imago Dei*: the image of God written into humanity.

While thousands of individuals could have been featured in this book, we have pared it back to one hundred. Your favorite hero of the faith might not be included. But hopefully you'll meet God through individuals you've not yet heard of. As you discover one saint, I'll introduce you to others who have inspired them and who they've inspired.

Method

The portraits in these pages aren't traditional Orthodox icons, although some Orthodox believers are featured and some are done in the style of such icons. If Orthodox icons act as sacred windows for encountering the divine, these portraits act as mirrors and windows, revealing our humanity as much as our desire to behold God.

They're also not traditional icons in terms of craft—the writing of an icon with egg tempera and gold leaf on panel—but rather woodcuts and linocuts. Creating a block print is labor-intensive, time-consuming, and meditative. My process has remained relatively consistent since I picked up a gouge nearly thirty years ago. First, I envision a composition in my imagination, and then I draw it to scale. I then transfer it in reverse to the block's surface, and then carve it using various U- and V-shaped gouges. After that, I roll an oil-based ink onto the surface, choose a paper, and then crank them both by hand through a printing press. Once the image is printed, I use watercolor to fill in the additional white space. This type of printmaking, all done by hand and using colored inks, dates back to the tenth century. The printing press was invented—along with using multiple blocks and movable type—in the fifteenth century to speed up the process.

There's something sacred about art making. It's meditative and prayerful, and it forces me to slow down. "In prayer and stillness before icons, we see the incarnational light," writes Linette Martin in *Sacred Doorways*. In the quiet of my studio, listening to sacred music, I become centered on God. Each detail that gets carved away summons "light" from the initial black block. The words that emerge become my prayers, and the human face that looks back at me reflects Christ the Divine.

Meditations

Visio divina, or "sacred seeing," is a form of prayer in which the viewer meditates on an image and allows God to speak through it. As an artist, I hope to offer you a different perspective or angle that you hadn't considered before. I hope to help you see in sacred ways.

Each entry contains a visual image and written meditation, Scripture passage, and brief prayer. The short meditation that accompanies each portrait offers a virtue, spiritual discipline, or concept that might benefit your walk of faith. You can ponder the stories of these followers of Christ through image and word, finding sacred doorways or windows leading to spiritual truth and encounters with God. You could use the prayer that frames each portrait as a breath prayer for the day, or you could take the book with you and gaze at a portrait during a short pause in your schedule.

The combined meditations offer roughly three months of daily devotions, if you choose to read one a day, from cover to cover. They are alphabetized according to the virtue or spiritual practice associated with them. You'll also find portraits of the Madonna and Child and of Jesus Christ done in the style of traditional Orthodox icons: the *Hodegetria* (Mother Mary holding the Christ child and gesturing toward him as the source of salvation) and *Pantocrator* (Jesus Christ shown as Ruler of all, the Sustainer of the world). In the material at the back of the book, you'll find reading guides for Advent and Christmas devotions and Lenten and Easter devotions and an index of the mystics and saints included in the book. Together, the lives of the saints and mystics in this book point toward Christ.

Ultimately, these mystics can inspire and equip us while giving us hope for our faith journey. Our prayer lives are enriched by the landscapes they've navigated, the adversities they've overcome, and the divine light that shines through them. They are part of the great cloud of witnesses who show us the way. They reveal all the ways that, as St. Martin de Porres reminds us, everything can be a prayer!

DOROTHY DAY (1897–1980) Activism

Share your food with the hungry . . . provide the poor wanderer with shelter—when you see the naked . . . clothe them.

—Isaiah 58:7

Activist Dorothy Day set out to change the world—one act of mercy at a time. Whether feeding the hungry, caring for the sick, or walking the picket lines, she took seriously Christ's admonition to service. Never one to back away from political issues, Dorothy championed voting rights while keeping one foot squarely in both parties. And she never voted. She was a member of the kingdom of heaven!

In 1933, Day and Peter Maurin started the *Catholic Worker* newspaper in New York City. The striking graphic block prints of Ade Bethune and Fritz Eichenberg and the stories and articles addressed Christian hospitality, social justice, the peace movement, and care for the poor. Day asks, "The greatest challenge of the day is: How to bring about a revolution of the heart?" She did this through education and example.

Jesus tells a parable about a king who empathizes with everyone in his kingdom. He commends those who feed and care for the hungry, stating, "Whatever you did for one of the least of these brothers and sisters of mine, you did for me" (Matt 25:40).

Day was driven by her strong convictions. Wherever she saw injustice, she took it upon herself to remedy the situation by peaceful means. She was imprisoned seven times, the last time at age seventy-five.

Activism doesn't necessarily place us in a position to be arrested, although it can. Signing a petition, boycotting corporations that act unjustly, writing to a politician, attending peaceful protests, and serving meals at a soup kitchen all realign the world with God's kingdom. "There is plenty to do for each one of us," Day readily admits, "working on our own hearts, changing our own attitudes, in our own neighborhoods."

What might the revolution of the heart look like today?

Suffering Servant, grant me the courage to take that first step into service. So many needs can be overwhelming, but I have something to offer. Guide me in ways that I can be a blessing to others. Help me to say, with Dorothy Day, "The only solution is love." Amen.

I really only Love God as much as I Love the Person I Love the Least
DOROTHY DAY

SATOKO KITAHARA (1929–1958) Assimilation

In Christ all the fullness of the Deity lives in bodily form.

—Colossians 2:9

Jesus became one of us. It was the ultimate act of assimilating into humanity. Just shy of incarnation, Satoko Kitahara took the plunge to do just that in the post–World War II slums of Tokyo, Japan. But it was a gradual process.

Satoko was from an aristocratic family in Tokyo and lived with her parents in an upscale neighborhood. Through a series of events, Satoko discovered Christianity, filling a longing within her. She was baptized, and shortly after, while praying for a place to serve others, she found her answer through a tall, bearded Franciscan named Brother Zeno, a companion of Maximilian Kolbe. He befriended Satoko and took her under his wing.

Satoko began traveling the short distance to a slum known as Ants Town, where she ministered to families displaced and made homeless by the war. It was what you would expect, writes a biographer: "Vagrants sleeping in cardboard boxes on winter nights, children with a tiny square of thin mat in subways, women who have to hire out their bodies to get a meal."

Satoko began to mentor the children, offering her services as best she could. Her efforts earned her the title "Mary of Ants Town." Like St. Paul, she became "all things to all people so that by all possible means [she] might save some."

When she contracted tuberculosis, her family wanted her hospitalized. Satoko, however, chose at this time to step down from her place of privilege and fully assimilate into Ants Town, living among the people. "If the good Lord wants to cure me, I am waiting here in Ants Town," Satoko said. "I do believe it is here he wants me to be, with my family."

Humble Christ, by taking on human flesh and the very nature of a servant, you became one of us. May I become all things to all people. Help me extend this love creatively to everyone, for you've chosen everyone to be in your family. Amen.

Do not fear, for I am with you; do not be dismayed, for I am your God.

—Isaiah 41:10

Nicolas Herman, known as Brother Lawrence of the Resurrection, was a humble Carmelite monk living in Paris. A self-described "clumsy oaf," Lawrence cooked at the monastery—a job he hated—and later mended sandals.

He was not a theologian, but after Lawrence passed away, some of his letters were published in a book titled *The Practice of the Presence of God*.

The spiritual insight Lawrence presents boils down to this: God is always there, and God always cares. "We need only to recognize God intimately present with us to address ourselves to Him every moment," he insists. This methodless method is an awareness and sensitivity developed toward the Holy Spirit.

"We can do little things for God. I turn the cake that is frying on the pan, for love of God," Lawrence confides. Amid the endless clamor of pots and pans, Lawrence found solace. In the simplicity of a grateful word or a loving thought directed heavenward, he found peace. "A little lifting up the heart suffices," he says. "A little remembrance of God, one act of inward worship."

Our workdays are cluttered with tasks and responsibilities, and sometimes we realize, suddenly, that we have been on autopilot. What would it mean to "retire" with God in the center of our souls, as Brother Lawrence invites?

Lawrence encourages us to redirect our thoughts toward God. We can become aware of the God who dwells in the "oratory of our heart."

O Beloved of my heart, I'm grateful that you will never leave me nor forsake me. You stick closer than a brother—closer than my breath and heartbeat. I take comfort in this. Keep me aware of your gentle presence through my waking hours, and blanket me while I sleep. Amen.

I KEEP MYSELF RETIRED WITH HIM IN THE DEPTH OF CENTER OF MY SOUL
Brother Lawrence

For we were all baptized by one Spirit so as to form one body—whether Jews or Gentiles, slave or free—and we were all given the one Spirit to drink.

—1 CORINTHIANS 12:13

Pentecost has occurred, Stephen has been stoned to death, and Saul is persecuting followers of the Way. Meanwhile, St. Philip is being Spirit-led south, out of Jerusalem and into Gaza.

Philip is walking along the road when an Ethiopian eunuch—a man in charge of the queen's treasury—passes by in a chariot. From ancient tradition, we know his name to be Djan Darada. The man is reading from the scroll of Isaiah: "He was led like a sheep to the slaughter, and as a lamb before its shearer is silent, so he did not open his mouth. In his humiliation he was deprived of justice. Who can speak of his descendants? For his life was taken from the earth" (Acts 8:32–33).

Philip jogs alongside the man and asks whether he understands the portion he's reading. Djan Darada invites Philip into the chariot to explain. Apparently, Philip does a good job, because as they pass by a body of water, the eunuch asks, "Look, here is water. What can stand in the way of my being baptized?" (Acts 8:36).

John the Baptist baptized Jesus in the Jordan River. Baptism represents a purification and cleansing from an old lifestyle in favor of a new direction. Following the resurrection of Christ, baptism had new meaning: St. Paul writes, "We were therefore buried with him through baptism into death in order that, just as Christ was raised from the dead through the glory of the Father, we too may live a new life" (Rom 6:4).

After Djan's baptism, the men part ways: Philip onto his next assignment, Djan south through Egypt, no doubt sharing his experience with those he encounters. Djan found his salvation the day his old life drowned. He went home rejoicing.

Ocean of Love, I humbly submerge myself in the waters of your grace. Ripen the fruits of my spiritual life as I emerge from the baptismal waters and into the sunlight of new life. Amen.

DJAN DARADA

But I am like an olive tree flourishing in the house of God.

—Psalm 52:8

Catholic environmentalist Wangari Maathai was disturbed by the disappearing forests in her native Kenya. She began taking active measures to counteract the destruction. It was a simple concept: plant a tree! Out of her initial sowing of that seed grew the Green Belt Movement: thousands of women planting millions of trees. "We owe it to ourselves and to the next generation to conserve the environment," Maathai asserts, "so that we can bequeath our children a sustainable world that benefits all."

Planting trees soon became a political issue. Maathai found herself up against a capitalist system of big business and greed. Planting trees would have been a nonissue, she said, except that misgovernance and environmental degradation go hand in hand. Maathai was repeatedly imprisoned as she became more vocal. She made giant strides with earth-friendly solutions long before sustainability was in vogue.

Maathai knew that we demonstrate our love for God through our love for God's creation. She was interested not just in planting trees but also solving problems of "malnutrition, scarcity of clean water, topsoil loss . . . why the infrastructure was falling apart." The Green Belt Movement grew into something significant, reaching far and wide and expanding outside the Kenyan borders.

We can "love ourselves by loving the earth," Maathai states. Together we can make a huge impact by doing small acts such as recycling, reducing water usage, conserving energy, and choosing nontoxic cleaning supplies. Together we can follow the example of Maathai and bequeath to our children a world where forests abound.

O Great Creator, I am blessed by the beauty around me—the lush vegetation and the diversity of the animal kingdom. Thank you for the ever-greening forests, the majestic mountains, and the crystal clear waters. Guide me in ways to care for your creation. Amen.

WE CAN LOVE OURSELVES BY LOVING THE EARTH
WANGARI
MAATHAI

Be perfect, therefore, as your heavenly Father is perfect.

—Matthew 5:48

Perfectionists can be unhealthy. The critical gaze with which they pick apart their own flaws moves outward to judge others. So what is Jesus getting at when he tells us to "be perfect"?

The Greek word τέλειοι, translated as "perfect" in Matthew 5:48, can be defined as an undivided heart, or complete spiritual maturity. John Wesley, the founder of the renewal movement known as Methodism, understood Christian perfection simply as "loving God with all our heart." He acknowledges that "absolute perfection belongs not to man, nor to angels, but to God alone."

Wesley's definition of perfection was quite different, however, in his early years. He and his brother Charles were part of a group known as the "Holy Club" at Oxford. The group was required to perform all religious duties: praying, studying, community service, and communion.

One evening in May 1738, he walked into a worship service on Aldersgate Street. All his striving for perfection, as we typically define it, fell by the wayside. "I felt my heart strangely warmed," he confessed.

From that day, Wesley wasn't so concerned about fulfilling religious rituals for their own sake or to earn God's favor. God already loved him just as he was, he concluded. Echoing St. Paul, Wesley preaches, "By justification we are saved from the guilt of sin and restored to the favor of God. By sanctification, we are saved from the power and root of sin and restored to the image of God." The perfection he sought and wished for, for himself and others, started and ended with love. "Love is the highest gift," he proclaims!

What if we started and ended with love too? What if by loving God, we, too, could find our hearts strangely warmed?

Son of a thousand suns, burn a fire in my soul that can't be extinguished: a fire of love that warms those around me and melts hardened hearts of ice. Fill me with a perfect love. Amen.

LORD, IN YOUR PRESENCE THERE IS NO NIGHT, IN THE LIGHT OF YOUR FACE IS PERPETUAL DAY
John Wesley

ORIGEN ADAMANTIUS (185–253) Christocentrism

For I resolved to know nothing while I was with you except Jesus Christ and him crucified.

—1 CORINTHIANS 2:2

Jesus once made a stunning claim to the Pharisees: "You study the Scriptures diligently because you think that in them you have eternal life. These are the very Scriptures that testify about me" (John 5:39–40). The ancient Hebrew writings, he told them, pointed to himself!

When it comes to interpreting Scripture, we face a daunting task. Christocentrism—the placing of Christ at the center of any given idea or act—can give us a key. What would it mean to read the Bible through the lens of Jesus? The theologian and ascetic Origen Adamantius interpreted Scripture and built his theology on this perspective: the crucified Christ.

Origen's intention was this: "The right way of understanding Scripture is to observe the rule and discipline which was delivered by Jesus Christ to the apostles and which they delivered in succession to their followers who teach the Church."

Origen wanted to understand the apparent contradictions between the God portrayed in the Hebrew Scriptures and the God revealed in the New Testament. "Show us the Father," Philip implores, perhaps wanting Christ to reveal a God who hurls down fire on command (John 14:8–9). "Anyone who has seen me has seen the Father," Jesus responds. Christ is merciful, self-sacrificing, humble, and loving: the Lion of Judah is a lamb, slain. The Father is exactly like the Son!

The Beatitudes, the Sermon on the Mount, the parables: these seem counterintuitive. But living according to Christ's words allow us to gaze on the "blessings to come," as Origen writes. "The aim for which we hope is that so far as it can happen we may be made participants in the divine nature by imitating Him," he instructs. So be it!

Thank you, Jesus, for revealing the nature of the Father, and your ability to love selflessly. A life lived with your heart and mind is a beautiful life. Let this magnificent kingdom come on earth as it is in heaven. Amen.

OPEN OUR EYES TO GAZE, NOT ON PRESENT REALITIES, BUT ON THE BLESSINGS TO COME
XLII
Origen Adamantius

So in Christ we, though many, form one body, and each member belongs to all the others.

—ROMANS 12:5

Lutheran pastor and theologian Dietrich Bonhoeffer watched in horror as leaders in the church swore allegiance to Hitler and the nation. Bonhoeffer remained a staunch objector to the Nazi regime. His loyalty to Christ and the church was unwavering. Consequently, he was imprisoned and eventually hanged.

In the years leading up to his imprisonment, Bonhoeffer led an underground seminary to train pastors in the Confessing Church tradition and wrote many books. One of his most important was *Life Together*, about Christian community. In it, he states, "Every member serves the whole body, either to its health or to its detriment." We each bring individual gifts and talents. These might serve the body directly or those outside the faith community.

But what of the one who is unable to offer much by way of visible talents? In contrast to Nazi ideology, Bonhoeffer states, "The elimination of the weak is the death of fellowship." He continues, "In a Christian community, everything depends upon whether each individual is an indispensable link in a chain." The marginalized are exceptional components in God's purposes.

St. James makes it clear that whether rich and strong or poor and weak, we all have a place in the Lord's house. Bonhoeffer concurs: "The mystery of our life together is that all of us can make a contribution providing we have a heart that seeks to serve."

The church community is composed of imperfect people, so an open, forgiving, and loving spirit is necessary. "The person who loves their dream of community will destroy community, but the person who loves those around them will create community," he adds.

Contemporary life, for many, involves loneliness: a life apart from others. What would it mean to live life together? To live together in the light that is God? Bonhoeffer writes, "Common prayers, sharing, encouragement, giving, ministry, and hospitality are some of the elements of such a life together."

Holy Trinity, we are all part of the great cloud of witnesses. We've been woven into a beautiful tapestry that you've designed. Thank you for the body of Christ. Amen.

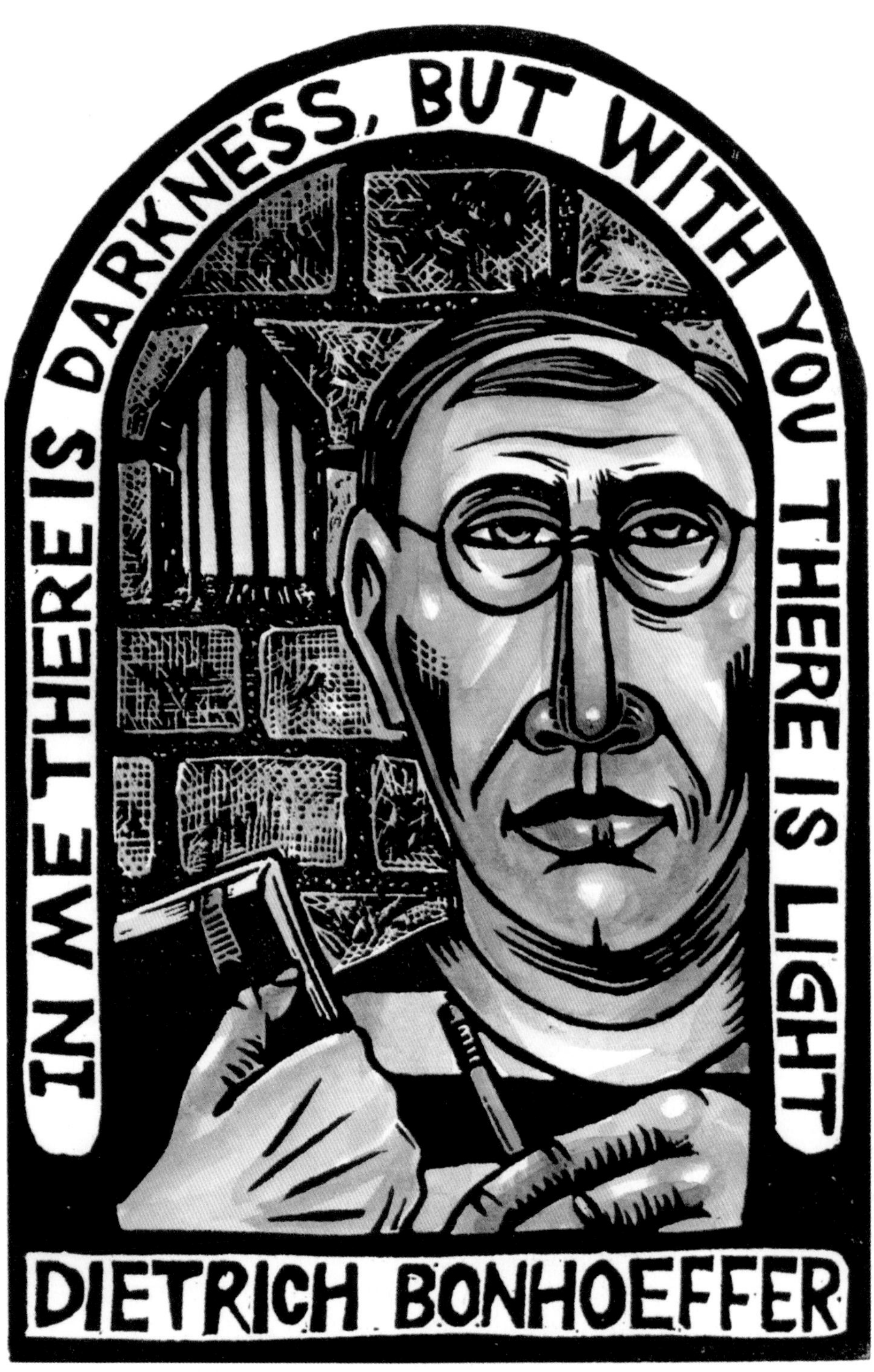
IN ME THERE IS DARKNESS, BUT WITH YOU THERE IS LIGHT
DIETRICH BONHOEFFER

Praise be to . . . the Father of compassion and the God of all comfort, who comforts us in all our troubles, so that we can comfort those in any trouble with the comfort we ourselves receive from God.

—2 CORINTHIANS 1:3–4

The mystic Mechthild of Magdeburg overcame a serious illness late in life. Mechthild was a Beguine, an order of Catholic women that began in the thirteenth century and that was known for their voluntary poverty and religious devotion. During her illness, she saw visions that moved her to write. The poetic love language that emerged became the book *The Flowing Light of the Godhead.* It featured accounts of mystical encounters, dialogues, and prayers, many of an erotic nature akin to the Song of Songs.

Mechthild wasn't afraid to speak out against corrupt clergy or address complex issues. She viewed God's justice not as vengeance wrought but compassion administered. "If you love the justice of Jesus Christ," she writes, "you will seek to do compassion."

"Compassion means that if I see my friend and my enemy in equal need, I shall help them both equally," Mechthild confesses. Compassion was to be administered freely, because God is love. According to Mechthild, we are to "seek and find the stranger, the broken, the prisoner, and comfort them and offer them our help."

Our inclination is to determine who is worthy of our compassion and who is not. Christ challenges this limited viewpoint many times, including in Luke 6:32–33, in which he suggests that it's easy to love those who love us. True compassion is a lot harder.

Compassion moved Jesus to feed and heal people indiscriminately—whether a blind Jewish man or a Roman centurion's servant. The writings of St. Paul and St. Peter admonish us to "clothe" ourselves with this same attribute.

Imagination helps us to enter another's experience. Then the Holy Spirit—who Mechthild called "the compassionate outpouring of the Creator and the Son"—offers creative solutions to administer this healing.

O Compassionate One, you've extended your healing hand to me. You've welcomed me with open arms. From this wellspring of abundant mercy I've received, let it flow freely to friend and foe alike. Amen.

draw me up to you then I shall be pure & radiant
Mechthild of Magdeburg

Truly you are a God who has been hiding himself. —Isaiah 45:15

We don't know who wrote *The Cloud of Unknowing*, a spiritual English text on contemplative prayer. And perhaps that anonymity is fitting. "Nobody's mind is powerful enough to grasp who God is," the medieval writer suggests about the unknowability of God; "we can only know him by experiencing his love."

This approach, known as the *via negativa*, strives to experience God rather than understand God; it limits descriptions of God to what God is *not*. In contemplation, we surrender to the mystery, to the ineffable: that which is unknown by both intellect and imagination. Trying to grasp eternity—a God with no beginning and no end—boggles the brain: this is to be expected with our finite minds.

And yet God desires to be revealed to us. A balance between the *kataphatic* (the revealed God) and the *apophatic* (the mystery of God) is healthy. We can know the love of God through the sacrificial Christ while still acknowledging our limitations of fully grasping God—I Am Who I Am. Our most significant insight into the character of God is Christ—God incarnate. Through contemplating Christ's selfless, sacrificial act on the cross, we can find that God is revealed.

"God is love," St. John writes in 1 John 4:8. If there is one thing the author of *The Cloud of Unknowing* knows, it's this! Once this statement of faith is settled, we can enter God's presence without fear or shame. We can enter into contemplation.

The writer encourages us to "Lift up [our] heart to God with a gentle stirring of love." Drawing near to the Divine, we rest in the silence and "focus on him alone . . . nothing but him." We release all else: burdens, thoughts, anxieties, insights.

In contemplation, we shift our gaze to the Mystery, the Source, the Creator. All our focus comes down to this: we become present to be with the Presence.

O Mysterious One, you are known and unknown. Yet we are made in your image. I come to you, fully present, ready to immerse in your river of love, to experience you, and to receive what you have to offer. Amen.

You make what is beyond brightness secretly to shine in all that is most dark
CLOUD of UNKNOWING

Be strong and courageous; do not be afraid; do not be discouraged, for the Lord your God is with you wherever you go.

—Joshua 1:9

It was December 1, 1955, when a Black woman on a bus in Montgomery, Alabama, chose to remain in her seat. This incident became the spark that would ignite the Montgomery Bus Boycott and set the stage for the civil rights movement.

Rosa Parks's faith in Christ gave her the impetus and courage to take a stand—or a seat—for justice. "Faith in God was never the question . . . it was the answer," writes Douglas Brinkley of Parks. "The teachings of Jesus Christ had convinced her instead, as they had Martin Luther King, Jr., that a heart filled with love could conquer anything, even bigotry."

Parks had long advocated for Black women who experienced sexual violence. During Jim Crow, legal definitions of rape only applied to white women. White men had used rape to terrorize Black women for centuries, and it was this hostile environment that the lion-hearted Parks entered, investigating survivors' stories and seeking justice. Those women who filed reports were harassed, intimidated, and eventually witnessed the perpetrators being set free by all-white male juries.

Yet there comes a time for David to stand up to Goliath, for Moses to defy Pharaoh, and for Rosa to take a seat against white supremacy. The costs were great: she would lose her job, as would her husband. Continually harassed, they moved less than two years later. But from her new home in Detroit, she still worked for justice. In 1996, she received the Presidential Medal of Freedom, and in 1999, the Congressional Gold Medal.

May we all learn the wisdom of Parks's words: "You must never be fearful about what you are doing when it is right."

God of justice, right the wrongs of a broken system, a system built on a faulty foundation. Brick by brick, tear it down! Then construct this building on the foundation of love and equality; a foundation of goodwill and kindness. Amen.

God did
away with all my fear
ROSA PARKS

I have filled him with the Spirit of God, with wisdom, with understanding, with knowledge and with all kinds of skills.

—Exodus 31:3

The first sentence of Genesis tells us that in the beginning, God created. Creativity is the initial thing God reveals. We're made in God's image, and creativity is ingrained in our DNA. This harmonious chord unites us to the cosmos and all created things.

Hildegard of Bingen was a one-woman explosion of creativity. Living in the Rhine River valley of Germany, she wrote poetry, composed music, and oversaw the production of sacred art. This monastic abbess also authored books on botany, biology, and medicine while advising authority figures in spiritual and political matters.

Hildegard was able to tap into communication with the divine Creator. "The Word is living, being, spirit, all verdant greening, all creativity," she acknowledges. This Word began to empower her with visions at age forty-two. Unable to contain the Spirit, she manifested *viriditas*, a word she used frequently to describe the greening, fertile, creating power of the Divine.

"There is the music of Heaven in all things," Hildegard observes. The ethereal qualities of her music elevate the soul while ushering in the Spirit. One observer writes that her "musical brilliance shines brightest [in] the sublimity of the liturgical poetry that accompanies it."

We long to tap into this creativity in all that we do. Whether cooking, gardening, decorating, painting, dancing, or another activity, we reflect God by developing creatively.

Incorporating creativity into our endeavors demands risk. If we are feathers on the breath of God, as Hildegard writes, in which direction might we be taken? "God's grace rewards not only those who never slip, but also those who bend and fall," Hildegard writes. "So sing!"

Lighter of the stars, you've made all things beautiful in their time. From the tiniest snowflake to the Milky Way, your creativity abounds. May my life reflect your creativity. Like Hildegard, may I weave the arts and all things beautiful and holy into my days. Amen.

THUS AM I, A FEATHER ON THE BREATH OF GOD
Hildegard of Bingen

Yet to all who did receive him, to those who believed in his name, he gave the right to become children of God.

—JOHN 1:12

Macarius was a camel driver and thief before he began searching for God and his true self. Eventually he founded a community southwest of Alexandria, which survives to this day as the Coptic Orthodox Monastery of St. Macarius the Great, in Egypt.

A brother once asked Macarius for a word. With wit, Abba Macarius gets to the root of our problems: attachment to the opinions of others. "Go to the cemetery and abuse the dead," is how the story goes in *The Sayings of the Desert Fathers.*

> The brother went there, abused them, and threw stones at them; then he returned and told the old man about it. The latter said to him, "Didn't they say anything to you?" He replied, "No." The old man said, "Go back tomorrow and praise them." So the brother went away and praised them, calling them, "Apostles, saints and righteous men." He returned to the old man and said to him, "I have complimented them." And the old man said to him, "Did they not answer you?" The brother said no. The old man said to him, "You know how you insulted them and they did not reply, and how you praised them and they did not speak; so you too if you wish to be saved must do the same and become a dead man."

It's hard not to react to what others say about us, whether negative or positive. But Macarius encourages us to find our acceptance in Christ alone. He helps us pray that God's knowledge and will and mercy prevail.

Henri Nouwen states, "As long as we are still wondering what other people say or think about us and trying to act in ways that will elicit a positive response, we are still victimized and imprisoned."

Ultimately, attachment to Christ requires detachment from all that tries to define us.

All-encompassing Creator, I detach from that which entangles and snares, from regrets and sorrows, from dark and hidden places; I fall ever deeper into your abyss of acceptance. Amen.

Lord as you know, & as you will, have mercy
abba Macarius

FANNIE LOU HAMER (1917–1977) Determination

Is not this the kind of fasting I have chosen: to loose the chains of injustice and untie the cords of the yoke, to set the oppressed free and break every yoke?

—Isaiah 58:6

Civil rights activist Fannie Lou Hamer knew hard times. A Mississippi sharecropper's daughter, she was picking cotton by the age of six. During attempts to vote, she was denied, harassed, beaten, humiliated, and shot at. Eventually, she got, in her famous words, "sick and tired of being sick and tired." This injustice set her course into a life of activism. Something needed to be done! Hamer finally realized, "You can pray until you faint, but unless you get up and try to do something, God is not going to put it in your lap." She cofounded the Mississippi Freedom Democratic Party, helped to organize Freedom Summer, and launched a Black farming collective and other economic enterprises.

One summer evening she and other Black people were riding a bus back home after another failed attempt to vote. A white police officer pulled over the bus and took the driver into custody. The vehicle was apparently "too yellow" and resembled a school bus. As the sun went down, eighteen African Americans awaited their plight on a Mississippi back road. Would they be arrested? Beaten? Lynched?

Then suddenly, from the back of the bus, Fannie Lou's voice cut through the silence. The same spirituals that gave courage to her grandmother, who had been enslaved, now brought comfort and courage to others. "Have a little talk with Jesus," she sang, the words from Rev. Cleavant Derricks's hymn filling the air: "Feel the little prayer wheel turning, / Feel a fire a-burning."

Hamer was determined to "untie the cords of the yoke," as the prophet Isaiah said. Her life created its own "prayer wheel," as the song says: a wheel of prayer, praise, and action.

God, my strength, grant me the determination to do right, seek justice, and defend the oppressed. Amen.

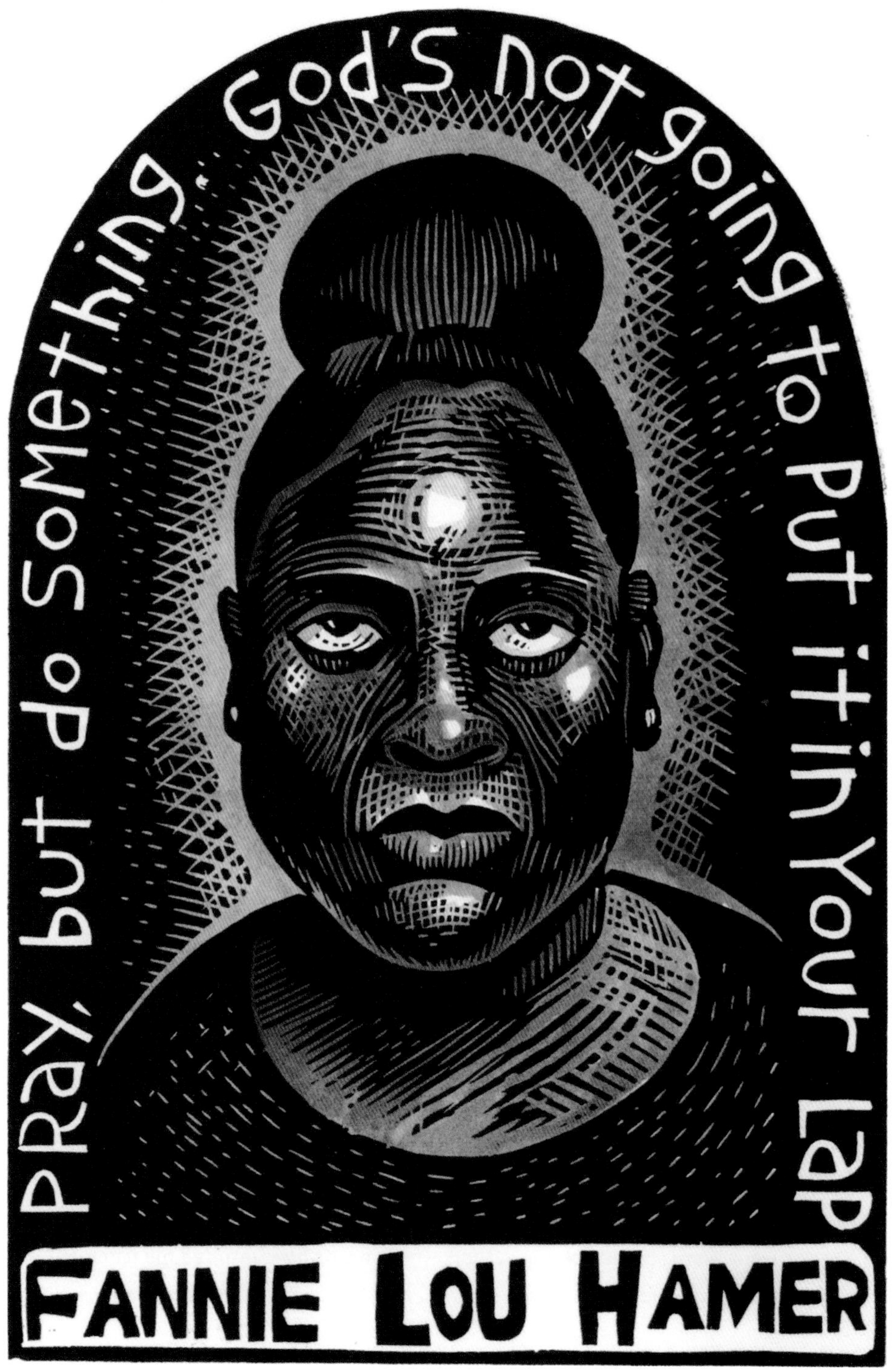
Pray, but do Something. God's not going to put it in your lap
FANNIE LOU HAMER

Follow God's example, as dearly loved children and walk in the way of love, just as Christ loved us.

—Ephesians 5:1–2

Thomas à Kempis, a monk living near Zwolle, Holland, transcribed manuscripts, copied the Bible, and wrote numerous books. *The Imitation of Christ* would become the second most widely published book, after the Bible.

This Christian devotional has been translated into over fifty languages and has influenced many religious scholars and poets. Ignatius of Loyola was so fond of the book that he read a chapter from it daily and often gave copies as gifts. John Wesley was said to always carry a copy, and he published an edited version for the Protestant believer called *The Christian Pattern.* Unfortunately, Thomas never had the opportunity to see the impact of his work, as he died the same year it was first published.

In these pages, Thomas encourages us to develop a life of silence and simplicity, grounded in humility, and fully lived in Jesus through prayer. Emphasizing spiritual formation and holiness, he writes, "Therefore, let your chief endeavor be to reflect on the life of Jesus Christ." The first three sections of the book offer practical advice under headings: "Useful Reminders for the Spiritual Life," "Suggestions Drawing One toward the Inner Life," and "Of Inner Comfort." The final section of the book, "On the Sacrament," addresses the mysteries of the Eucharist.

With its roots in late-medieval European culture, *The Imitation of Christ* tends toward dualistic thinking about body and spirit. Modern readers might find it quite legalistic. Yet if we read it with several filters in place, it can offer us helpful guidance. Thomas advises that when we read spiritual books, "let the love of simple truth, rather than the reputation or the authority of the author, motivate your reading."

What motivates your devotion? How might spiritual reading and writing illuminate the life of Jesus Christ?

Living Word, thank you for authors whose words have inspired me along my path of life. Guide me, Spirit of truth, for you are my Instructor. Amen.

O Light eternal, enlighten the inmost recesses of my heart
Thomas A Kempis

And the God of all grace, who called you to his eternal glory in Christ, after you have suffered a little while, will himself restore you and make you strong, firm and steadfast.

—1 PETER 5:10

Pandita Ramabai was born into a high-caste Hindu family, but she lost her parents and brother early in life when famine swept through India. Soon after that, she broke cultural mores and married beneath her, only to have her husband pass away less than two years later. She now lived with the stigma of having done something bad, either in this life or else one prior.

While still in her twenties, Ramabai traveled to Britain, where she encountered the gospel. She discovered something unique in this man, Jesus. Even though he lived in a patriarchal culture, he treated women with utmost respect and dignity. She confessed, "I realized after reading the fourth chapter of St. John's Gospel that Christ was truly the Divine Saviour he claimed to be, and no one but He could transform and uplift the downtrodden womenhood of India and of every land."

Ramabai returned to India and founded an organization in 1882 "to promote education among native women of India and the discouragement of child marriage." Seven years later she founded the Mukti Mission. *Mukti* means freedom, or salvation. Initially built to educate child widows, the program extended to include orphans, discarded children, and destitute women. She wished to educate and empower the women and girls while restoring their God-given dignity.

Ramabai spoke seven languages, including Sanskrit, the sacred Hindu language only to be known by men. She excelled at the language and was given the title *Pandita* for her fluency in Sanskrit—the only woman to have been awarded that title. At the end of her life, she would translate the Bible into her native tongue, Marathi.

Ramabai was convinced of her identity in Christ and that everyone had inherent dignity. Through the Mukti Mission, her impact in India continues to this day.

Compassionate Counselor, restore the dignity of women and children who have been trampled. As a mother hen, gather your chicks to places of safety, healing, and hope. Amen.

rama bai
no one but christ can
transform and lift
the downtrodden

And now these three remain: faith, hope and love. But the greatest of these is love.

—1 Corinthians 13:13

John Climacus was a monk at the Monastery of St. Catherine on Mount Sinai in Egypt. During his time as abbot, John wrote the spiritual classic *The Ladder of Divine Ascent*. While it was written by a monk for other monks, many laypersons have gleaned insight from the teachings. The devotional has become a favorite among Eastern Orthodox believers, who often read it during Lent.

While he uses the image of a ladder, Climacus isn't suggesting that the spiritual elite can somehow climb to heaven. Rather, he's promoting a lifestyle of purity and holiness once one is forgiven of sins. Each step on the ladder represents a discipline to exercise or a virtue to obtain.

For the monk, this begins by breaking away from the "world." And while a layperson isn't about to depart for the isolation of Sinai, the principle of separating oneself from a harmful environment is just as important. An alcoholic in recovery shouldn't be hanging out at the local bar, and a compulsive gambler should avoid the casino.

Building a life of self-control over our passions brings us to the top of the ladder, which is love. "Love, by its nature, is a resemblance to God," Climacus writes; its "character is to be a fountain of faith, an abyss of patience, a sea of humility." All the virtues, all the disciplines, and all the steps we climb are ultimately wrapped up in the package of love.

Love is to be practiced at all times. But we don't just miraculously excel at loving when we reach the summit. We exercise love at each step: fighting pride, selfishness, and slander. We wish to love more fully through acts of kindness and self-sacrifice. And we desire to minimize those things that distract us from love.

O Most High, thank you for climbing down the ladder of divine descent. I'm grateful for the forgiveness you offer, and for clothing me in your righteousness. Draw me upward toward love, empowering me with each step. Amen.

PRAY IN ALL SIMPLICITY
JOHN CLIMACUS

In your relationships with one another, have the same mindset as Christ Jesus . . . he humbled himself.

—PHILIPPIANS 2:5–8

For spiritual writer and priest Henri Nouwen, pursuing a radical Christian life was the ultimate priority. He came to describe this as "downward mobility." "Just as we came to see God in the downward way of Christ, so we will become conscious of truly being sons and daughters of God by becoming participants in this downward way, the way of the cross," Nouwen asserts. This upside-down kingdom is the polar opposite of the world's ways, where success is measured by how far one can climb up the ladder of riches, power, and prestige.

Nouwen relinquished a position at Harvard Divinity School in 1986, taking up residence as a mentor at a community for those with mental and physical disabilities. It was here that Nouwen found fulfillment. His final year there was recorded in his published journal, *The Road to Daybreak: A Spiritual Journey.*

In his book *The Selfless Way of Christ*, Nouwen points to the wilderness temptations Jesus faced as challenges that plague the church to this day: to be relevant, spectacular, and powerful. Jesus not only preached on these dangers but lived his life in opposition to them. The church in the West has come to see signs of upward mobility—job promotions, bigger houses, and fancier cars—as blessings from God. But these are merely the goals of the American consumer.

Nouwen invites us to step back and take a broader perspective. Rather than always grabbing for the gold ring, we can relinquish our desires and exchange them for God's will. We can choose the downward way.

Cruciform Christ, I relinquish to you—my loving caretaker and friend—the control of my life that I so desperately desire to hold onto. I will walk through the doors that you open, and not those of my own making. Amen.

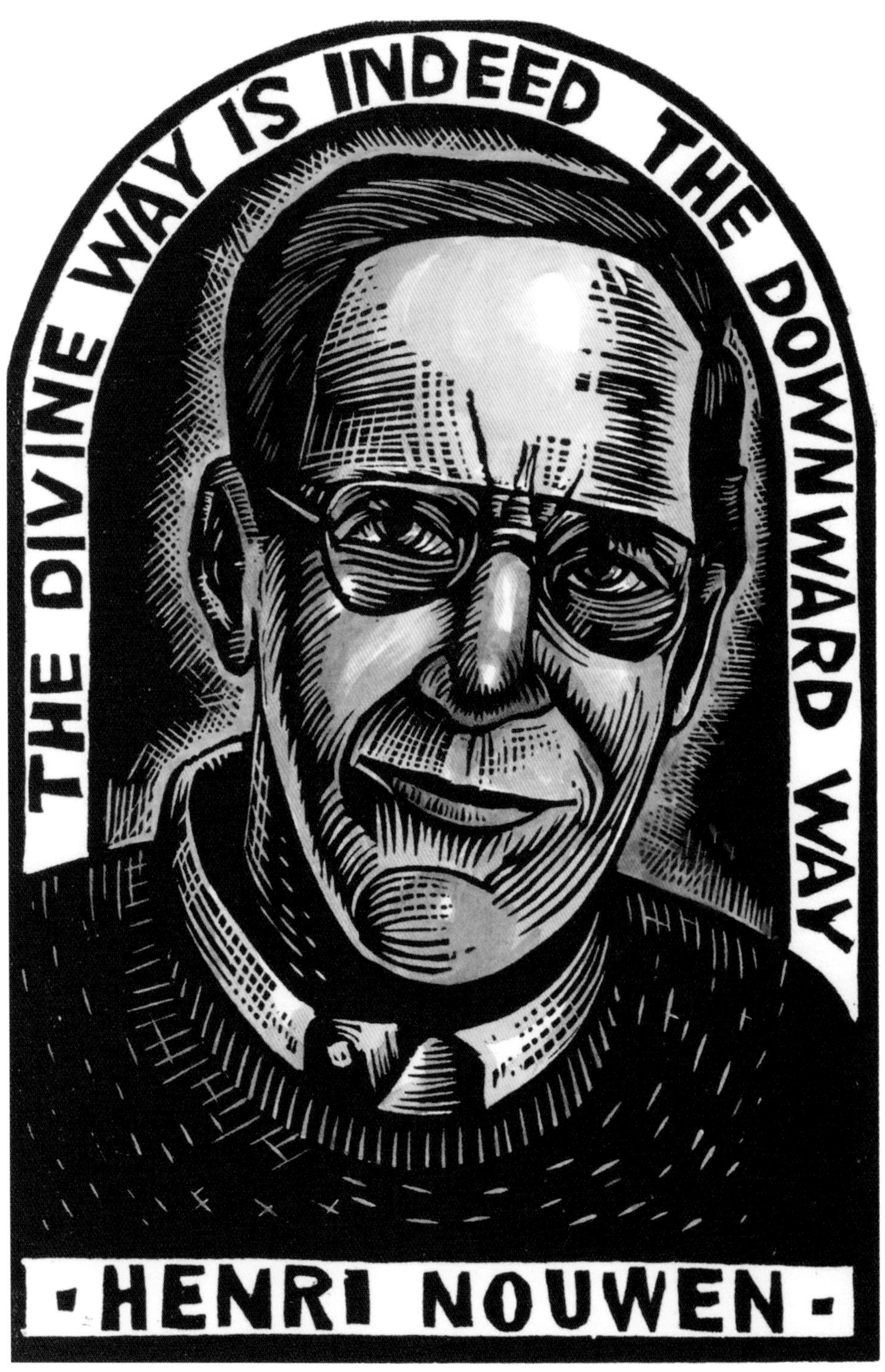
THE DIVINE WAY IS INDEED THE DOWNWARD WAY
HENRI NOUWEN

Jesus reached out his hand and touched the man. —LUKE 5:13

Empathy is the capacity to feel the pain of another, and it can take us to hard places. Serving the Black community in Selma, Alabama, in the early 1960s, Father Maurice Ouellet had befriended the Rev. Martin Luther King Jr. As a white Catholic, he invited the Black Protestant civil rights leader to hold meetings in his church in the days leading up to the march from Selma to Montgomery.

That didn't sit well with his superior. "While I am Bishop of Mobile, there will be no picketing by priests or nuns and no marching," Rev. T. J. Toolen would write.

Father Ouellet heeded the bishop's orders and didn't march the morning of May 7, 1965. As he stood on the steps of the Black parish he pastored, all the sirens in the city went off. "It was haunting," he said, "and I just knew something terrible had happened." It would come to be known as Bloody Sunday.

Father Ouellet made his way to the only "Negro" hospital in Selma. Inside, badly injured people waited for medical attention. Many white doctors refused to enter. A girl lay on the floor, her head bloodied. Oullet recalled, "Her eyes focused right into my face, and she said, 'Oh, Father, I hurt.'" He later wrote, "I wiped from my cheek the blood of Christ, that of a little girl, His Blood, her blood, as it poured from the side of her head cradled on my shoulder. Here was the uncomfortable Christ."

"We are called upon to continue the life of Christ now, not as we see fit," he said, "but as it is required by the needs of the rest of the Mystical Body."

Empathy is a way of encountering the One Father Ouellet called "the uncomfortable Christ." It helps us continue the life of Christ now.

Christ of compassion, give me the courage to encounter you when you show up in uncomfortable ways. Help me to imitate your life now, not as I see fit but as the needs of your body require. Amen.

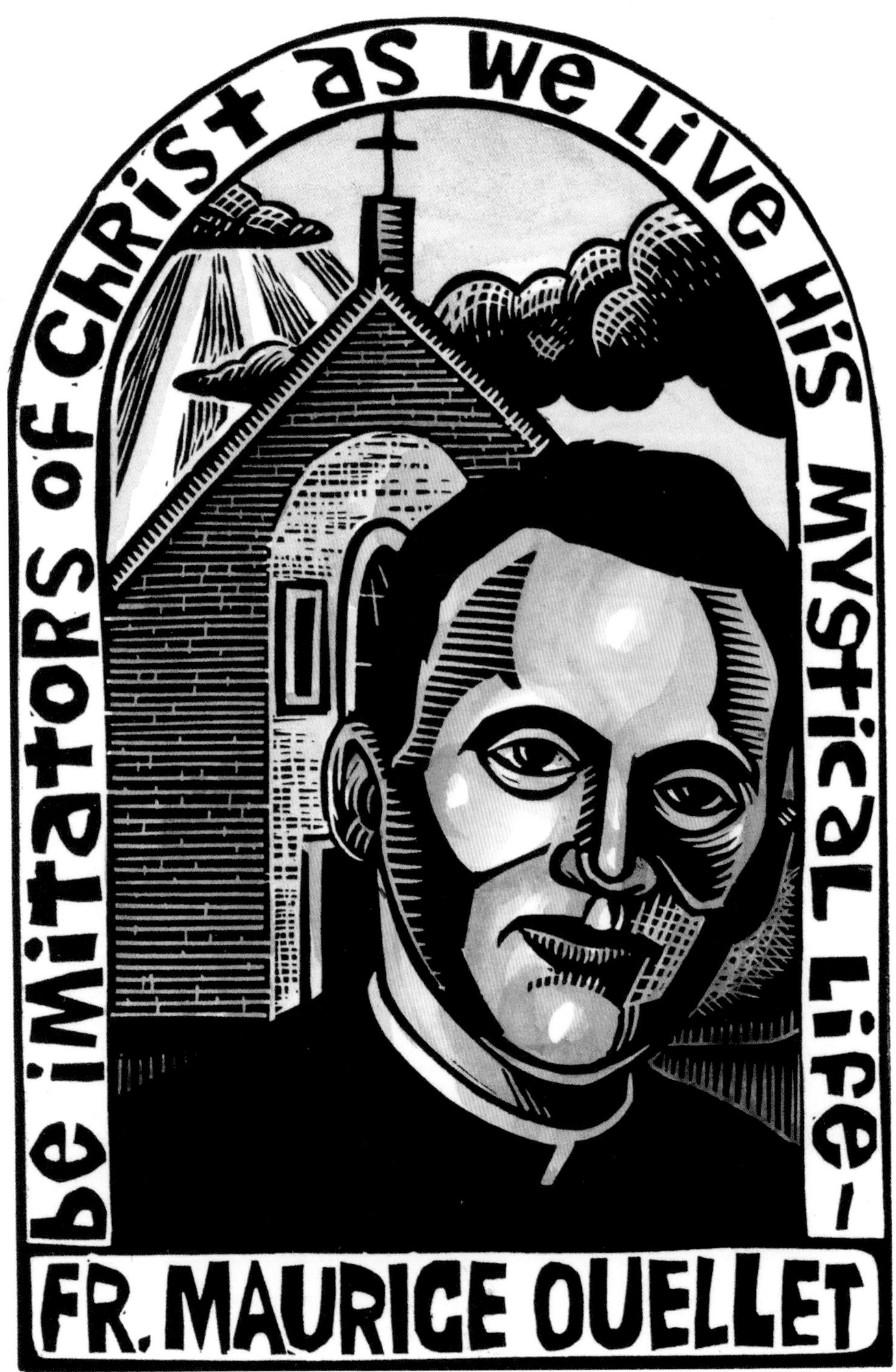
be imitators of Christ as we live His mystical life -
FR. MAURICE OUELLET

Therefore encourage one another and build each other up, just as in fact you are doing.

—1 THESSALONIANS 5:11

St. James writes of the dangers of the tongue. "Out of the same mouth come praise and cursing," he states. "My brothers and sisters, this should not be" (Jas 3:10). People often carry scars from derogatory comments inflicted by parents, teachers, or others close to them.

The Celtic Christian Hilda of Whitby was a gentle and encouraging teacher. She was a protégé of another sensitive leader, St. Aidan, the bishop of Lindisfarne. She founded the double monastery at Whitby, which supported the arts, music, and education. The monastery brought together men and women, who lived in separate quarters while sharing the same sanctuary. Hilda had a tender and nurturing relationship with the young religious. Those who knew her referred to her as Mother, according to St. Bede in his *Ecclesiastical History of the English People*.

The story goes that a young monk named Caedmon, a poet, composed hymns based on Scripture but was self-conscious about his singing. During the community's times of sharing and playing music, he would slip away to avoid being called on. Hilda, however, saw his talent, and she knew it came from God. So Hilda "encouraged him to stay at the monastery to learn the Bible stories and to create them into poetry and song," writes Rev. Brenda Warren. "Through this encounter with Hilda, Cædmon became the first English poet."

Words can't be rescinded. Choosing our words wisely is achieved by being "slow to speak" (Jas 1:19). If we let impatience or anger drive our remarks, we may regret it. But if we speak encouraging words, who knows what poetry might be born?

We can take to heart Hilda's final words on her deathbed, words with which she comforted her brothers and sisters: "Keep the peace of the gospel with one another and indeed with the entire world."

Face of Love, help me to be quick to listen and slow to speak. Use the words I do speak as salt and light, bringing encouragement to the hearts of all who hear them. Amen.

keep the peace of the
Hilda
of
Whitby
Gospel with one another

AMMA SYNCLETICA (?–350) Endurance

I have told you these things, so that in me you may have peace. In this world you will have trouble. But take heart! I have overcome the world.

—John 16:33

Amma Syncletica was one of three *ammas*, or desert mothers, recorded in the ancient *Apophthegmata Patrum*. Her family migrated from Macedonia to Alexandria, Egypt, in the third century to be part of a larger Christian community. After her parents died, Syncletica fled to the desert regions, where she lived consecrated to Christ. She lived as a solitaire, but many seekers came to her for spiritual advice.

Syncletica offers us this wisdom: "Those who put out to sea at first sail with a favorable wind; then the sails spread, but later the winds become adverse. Then the ship is tossed by the waves and is no longer controlled by the rudder. But when in a little while there is a calm, and the tempest dies down, then the ship sails on again. So it is with us, when we are driven by the spirits who are against us; we hold to the cross as our sail and so we can set a safe course."

Her years in self-imposed solitude can help us navigate our own isolation. During the years of the pandemic, many found themselves tempest-tossed. The crisis caught some off guard. Did God even care? Or was Jesus just asleep in the boat?

As storms gather on the horizon, sometimes all we can do is cling to the cross—the mast of suffering—and wait for the storm to pass. Stripped of superficial comforts and unanswered questions, we reach the point where we can honestly say, "I don't know!" We can take Amma Syncletica's advice, bringing us to a deeper trust and a stronger faith.

Compassionate One, the journey is long and endurance is needed. Although these trials are painful, I know adversity can produce good fruit; strengthen me and set me on a safe course. Amen.

WE HOLD TO THE CROSS AS OUR SAIL AND SO WE CAN SET A SAFE COURSE ✝
AMMA SYNCLETICA

JARENA LEE (1783–1864) Evangelism

Then I heard the voice of the Lord saying, "Whom shall I send? And who will go for us?" And I said, "Here am I. Send me!"

—Isaiah 6:8

A young Jarena Lee wished to preach in the newly formed African Methodist Episcopal (AME) Church. "There seemed to sound a voice which I thought I distinctly heard, and most certainly understood, which said to me, 'Go preach the Gospel!'" she stated. Jarena even confided her desire to its founder, Richard Allen. But he refused. Although Allen could see the need to separate from a Methodist denomination that exhibited anti-Blackness, he couldn't see his own gender bias. Would he be able to accept the prophetic words and divine calling of Black women?

Lee confronted Allen: "If the man may preach, because the Savior died for him, why not the woman, seeing he died for her also? Is he not a whole Savior, instead of a half one, as those who hold it wrong for a woman to preach, would seem to make it appear?"

It was a Sunday morning in 1817 when Jarena felt that burning in her bones again. When the preacher faltered midway through his sermon, she stood up immediately in the congregation and delivered the word of the Lord. "God made manifest his power," Lee would later write. AME founder Richard Allen, who sat in the congregation, was now fully convinced she was anointed.

From that day forth, Lee took to her new calling, becoming the first African American woman to preach the gospel publicly. Her travels, mostly on foot, took her thousands of miles from the slave state of Maryland to northern cities in the United States and Canada.

Preaching the gospel, Jarena Lee became a model for many who would come after her. Here we are. Send us!

God who seeks and saves, you have come to call and coax; to bind and heal; to welcome us all home. Empower me in my gifts, that I might be a benefit and blessing and share the good news with others. Amen.

Jarena Lee
the
love of
God, and
of his service
burned with a ve-
hement flame within me

JOHN THE BAPTIST (first century) Faith

Now faith is confidence in what we hope for and assurance about what we do not see.

—HEBREWS 11:1

The dark, dank cell where John the Baptist was imprisoned likely reflected his inner emotional state. The one who heard God affirm Jesus at his baptism; the one who confidently stated, "Behold, the Lamb of God, who takes away the sin of the world!" (John 1:29 ESV); the one who said, "He must become greater; I must become less" (John 3:30): this man was now having his own personal Gethsemane experience.

While John wasted away in prison, with no sign of revolt on the horizon, he asked his disciples to go ask Jesus a question: "Are you the one who was to come, or should we expect someone else?"

We all, like John the Baptist, want answers. In the Gospels, people ask Jesus 183 questions—and he answers three. In turn, he asks 307 questions!

Learning to live with hard questions instead of answers might not bring comfort. But it is the complexity and mystery of our faith. Dark nights of the soul will come for most of us. During those times, we often struggle with theology. To some degree, John expected a different outcome. With God on his side, how could he be sitting in prison? What sense can be made of the upside-down kingdom: strength in weakness, receiving in giving, life in death?

Before John was beheaded, he received an answer. His disciples returned to let him know that Jesus had said this: "The blind receive sight, the lame walk, those who have leprosy are cured, the deaf hear, the dead are raised, and the good news is preached to the poor" (Matt 11:5). While his life would still end soon, that message likely gave him hope. This was what the kingdom was all about all along! It was Jesus's mission statement.

John could now rest assured. Whatever was happening to him, whatever would happen, God was with him. Whatever will happen, God is with us.

Lamb of God, in my Gethsemane, in my own times of darkness or doubt, when pat answers don't quench my thirst, reassure me that you are my everything! Amen.

behold the lamb of god who takes away the sin of the world
John the baptist

I will give you a new heart and put a new spirit in you; I will remove from you your heart of stone and give you a heart of flesh.

—Ezekiel 36:26

Fasting—abstaining from that which pollutes the mind and controls the body—is a means to strengthen self-control. We might fast from food, or technology, or anything that threatens to annex our affection and allegiance. Feeding repeatedly on round-the-clock news, for example, can create a detrimental mindset until we begin to hate the very people Jesus sought to redeem—ourselves and others. Ultimately, what we choose to fill our heads with does affect our spiritual health!

Abba Poemen, when asked how we should fast, replied, "I think it better that one should eat every day, but only a little, so as not to be satisfied." He also offers us this sound advice: "The nature of water is soft, that of stone is hard; but if a bottle is hung above the stone, allowing the water to fall drop by drop, it wears away the stone," he said. "So it is with the word of God; it is soft and our heart is hard."

As we shift our gaze from the negative to the positive—from the fast to the thing the fast allows us to hunger for—a new reality comes into view. When we pray, praising and reflecting on God's goodness, and when we meditate on Scripture, poetry, or other spiritual writing, a soothing balm reaches our soul. As words drip into our hearts, we can allow them to soften and penetrate the dry cracks that have become cynical, controlling, or downright harmful.

Throughout our day, what are we consuming that might threaten to consume us? What are we allowing to fill our minds? Are we slowly building a calloused shell around our mind, sealing inside cynicism, fear, and hate? Or are we allowing the refreshing Word of God to drip into our hearts?

O Beloved, soothe with the salve of your words the dry, cracked ground of my hardened heart. Help me to long for you and your word. Amen.

dripping water pierces rock; God's repeated word penetrates hearts
abba poemen

They devoted themselves to the apostles' teaching and to fellowship, to the breaking of bread and to prayer. . . . All the believers were together and had everything in common.

—Acts 2:42, 44

During the tumultuous decades of the 1950s and 1960s, Clarence Jordan longed to transcend the social and racial mores of his time. He wanted to let people know the body of Christ is not segregated. So the white theologian and farmer, who would write the *Cotton Patch* series (a paraphrase of the New Testament) and help to found Habitat for Humanity, started Koinonia Farm, an interracial Christian community in Americus, Georgia. Together, Black and white people tried to follow the principles of the early church: nonviolently and distributing their wealth for the common good.

The community experienced harsh backlash. Many white people deemed interracial relationships a sin and frowned on school desegregation. Koinonia Farm was boycotted, threatened, and bombed several times. The local Ku Klux Klan organized a massive motorcade to drive to the farm to intimidate the members.

But what many white people in society and the church were unable to see was a love that didn't quit. "Love is not merely a weapon. It is not a strategy, and it may or may not work," Jordan acknowledged. "To do good to those who hate you is such stupendous folly that it cannot be expected to work. Love didn't work for Jesus."

Koinonia is the Greek word for "fellowship." And love is at the core of fellowship. It's something more profound than community, more than simply living in the same vicinity. Fellowship requires selflessness, generosity, trust, and vulnerability; it strives for forgiveness and mercy. The "stupendous folly" that is love doesn't always "work," according to common metrics of success, but it always hopes.

We must intentionally reach out to others different from us to be the body of Christ. "The crowning evidence that he lives is not a vacant grave," Jordan suggests, "but a spirit-filled fellowship. Not a rolled-away stone, but a carried-away church."

Holy Trinity, you are three, but you are one. Within you is fellowship. Help us to grasp the folly that is the truest form of love. Amen.

the only right that love has is the right to give itself
CLARENCE JORDAN

Seven times a day I praise you. —PSALM 119:164

St. Romuald was the founder of many monasteries and a monastic order in central Italy. Not only did he practice the communal *Benedictine Rule*; he formed his own short rule for the eremitical life. "Sit in your cell," he said, "and cast all memory of the world behind you."

The monk is called to prayer when the church bell rings. All other activity ceases, as communion with God is of the utmost importance. "Nothing is to be preferred to the work of God (prayer)," states St. Benedict in his *Rule*. Whether in a community or individually, this rhythm of prayer is the heartbeat of the body of Christ.

Most of us set aside three times daily to eat and nourish our physical bodies. So why not do the same for our spiritual health? The discipline of fixed-hour prayer—whether morning and evening, four times a day, or seven times a day—offers us a framework. With a steady diet of prayer throughout our day, whether written or spontaneous, we learn to "watch our thoughts," as Romuald says.

"Take every opportunity you can to sing the Psalms in your heart," Romuald instructs, "to understand them with your mind." Praying with the Psalms, or a prayer book such as *The Book of Common Prayer*, gives us words we can use—words of the human condition. You can pray any type of prayer in a fixed-hour way.

Such words are available to us when we don't know what or how to pray. We can say prayers that have been said for thousands of years. We can say prayers that Jesus prayed! When we pray, we join in community with the great cloud of witnesses: saints who have gone before and siblings in Christ worldwide.

Fixed-hour prayer can offer support for our faith. It is like a trellis, on which our prayer life can grow and blossom.

O Indwelling Presence, I don't always understand the power of prayer, words floating into thin air. But you prayed often and encouraged us to do the same. Bring me into the company of community of the saints in offering you praise. Amen.

WATCH YOUR THOUGHTS LIKE A GOOD FISHERMAN WATCHING FOR FISH
SAINT ROMUALD

Forgive as the Lord forgave you. —COLOSSIANS 3:13

Led by a vision, young St. Patrick traversed the lush green meadows and hills, making his way to the coast. For many days he traveled, avoiding contact with strangers, until he arrived at the harbor and saw the ship from his dream. Quickly securing passage, he offered a prayerful sigh of thanks as he boarded. Enslaved no more, Patrick was bound for his home in Britain!

One can hardly imagine what went through his head when God called him back to the place of his captivity. Now a bishop, he was sent there to share the good news of God's reconciliation. Patrick discovered the depth of God's love the day he stepped off the boat: standing on the Rock of Mercy, his heart enlarged to embrace all of Ireland.

Patrick later wrote in his *Confessions*, "After my many hardships and misfortunes, after such great difficulties and burdens, after my captivity and enslavement, after so many years living among the Irish, He should give me so great a grace in behalf of this nation of people—something that once, in my boyhood, I never dreamed nor could even hope for."

Forgiveness is a God-given gift. When that gift is exercised, there's no telling what's possible. Patrick's impact on the Emerald Isle would be undeniable; his name is associated with Ireland for all time.

When Peter asks Jesus how many times he must forgive, Jesus says seventy-seven. Forgiveness frees not just the perpetrators of wrongdoing but the survivors of it. St. Patrick found a way to forgive and to be free.

I arise today, through
God's strength to pilot me,
God's might to uphold me,
God's wisdom to guide me,
God's eye to look before me,
God's ear to hear me,
God's word to speak for me,
God's hand to guard me,
God's shield to protect me,
God's host to save me.
Amen.
(partial prayer, attributed to St. Patrick)

CHRIST WITH ME, BEFORE ME, BEHIND ME, IN ME, BENEATH & ABOVE ME
PATRICK of IRELAND

JOSEPHINE BAKHITA (1869–1947) Freedom

So if the Son sets you free, you will be free indeed. —JOHN 8:36

Josephine Bakhita was born in 1869 in what is now western Sudan. At a young age, she was kidnapped by Arab slave traders. Bakhita would soon discover the pain of being branded and receiving a whip to the back, and the indignity of being bought and sold. Enslaved by a Turkish general, she received numerous scars from the whip. In addition, she got branded with 114 scar tattoos—cuts filled with salt—to produce identification marks.

Bakhita eventually became the property of an Italian family. While they were on vacation, she was sent to be cared for by the Canossian Sisters in Venice. It was here that she came to understand divine love. "Those holy mothers instructed me with heroic patience and introduced me to that God who from childhood I had felt in my heart without knowing who He was," she later reflected. She had seen the sun and moon and stars. She knew that these beautiful, free things had a Creator.

When her enslavers returned, Bakhita refused to leave, and a legal battle ensued. The court, however, ruled in her favor. Slavery had been illegal before her birth in Sudan. Italian law did not recognize slavery, so Bakhita had never legally been a slave. That day she received her freedom. It was a freedom that, in many ways, she already had. She knew she had intrinsic dignity.

St. Josephine "is charged with showing to all the path of conversion," Pope Francis has stated, "which enables us to change the way we see our neighbors, to recognize in every other person a brother or sister in our human family and to acknowledge his or her intrinsic dignity in truth and freedom." She shows us what emanicipation looks like.

Christ who sets all people free, liberate us. Thank you for those like St. Josephine, who model for us true freedom. Thank you that I am definitely loved. Amen.

I
am
defi-
nitely
loved
Josephine
Bakhita

But when you give to the needy, do not let your left hand know what your right hand is doing, so that your giving may be in secret.

—Matthew 6:3–4

Few authentic sources exist about the life of St. Nicholas of Myra. But a ninth-century monk, Michael the Archimandrite, pieced together the following story.

There was a man from Patara, in modern-day Turkey, unable to provide dowries for his three daughters; this meant they would remain unmarried. Without any means of employment, a life of prostitution was in their future. It was the unfortunate plight of women in the culture at this time.

Nicholas heard of the young women's situation. Wanting to spare their dignity and save the family from public humiliation, he went to their house under cover of night and threw a small bag of gold coins through the open window. When the father discovered the bag, he immediately arranged a marriage for his first daughter.

After her wedding that evening, Nicholas threw a second bag through the same window, and the father discovered it the next morning.

After the second daughter was married, the father stayed awake until he caught St. Nicholas doing the same charitable act for the third daughter. The father thanked him profusely, while Nicholas ordered him not to tell anyone about the gifts.

This story became popular in ancient icons, paintings, and frescoes. Although the scenes may vary slightly, depending on time and place, Nicholas often wears a red-hooded cloak, while the daughters are shown in bed dressed in their nightgowns.

Over time, of course, St. Nicholas would morph into the more commercial Santa Claus. Still, the love language of gift-giving shows us a tangible picture of grace and generosity. In giving good gifts to others, we begin to mimic God.

Giver of all good gifts, my anticipation and excitement turn to joy when I peer into the manger on Christmas morning. May my life reflect your generosity in some small way, with my heart bringing warmth to thaw someone's cold winter night. Amen.

THE GIVER OF EVERY GOOD AND PERFECT GIFT HAS CALLED US TO MIMIC HIM
Nicholas of Myra

AIDAN OF LINDISFARNE (?–651) Gentleness

Let your gentleness be evident to all. —PHILIPPIANS 4:5

The Irish monk St. Aidan studied under the tutelage of St. Senan on Inis Cathaigh, off the west coast of Ireland. He traveled north, where he joined the Iona monastery. While he was there, missionaries returned from Northumbria, complaining of the crude and brutal people they had encountered. Aidan suggested they might have been too harsh with the new and potential converts. Begin by "giving them the milk of simple teaching," Aidan recommended. They were to nourish them with God's word until they could "follow the loftier precepts of Christ."

The monks agreed that Aidan should travel back and try his luck at ministry. As the newly appointed bishop, he settled on the tidal island of Lindisfarne. The island, reachable only at low tide, has now become a pilgrimage destination.

The gentle leader soon began a successful ministry that grew and flourished. St. Bede writes, "He taught nothing that he did not practice in his life among his brethren."

One story tells how King Oswin gave him a horse, despite Aidan's objections. The humble leader didn't want to have more wealth or look down on those he served. As he rode off, he came upon a beggar, and he decided to give the surprised man his horse. When King Oswin heard about it, he was furious and confronted the bishop. "Is that foal of a mare more dear to you than the Son of God?" Aidan responded. Oswin mulled over Aidan's response, knelt before him, and begged his forgiveness.

Having a gentle disposition can turn away wrath. The gentle and humble heart that beat inside Christ had also developed within Aidan. The virtue of gentleness spread, beginning to take root in those he encountered.

O Compassionate One, help me not be harsh with my words and actions but gentle and humble, not to break a bruised reed or snuff out a smoldering wick. I pray with St. Aidan, "As the tide draws the waters close in upon the shore, make me an island, set apart, alone with you, God, holy to you. Then, with the turning of the tide, prepare me to carry your presence to the busy world beyond." Amen.

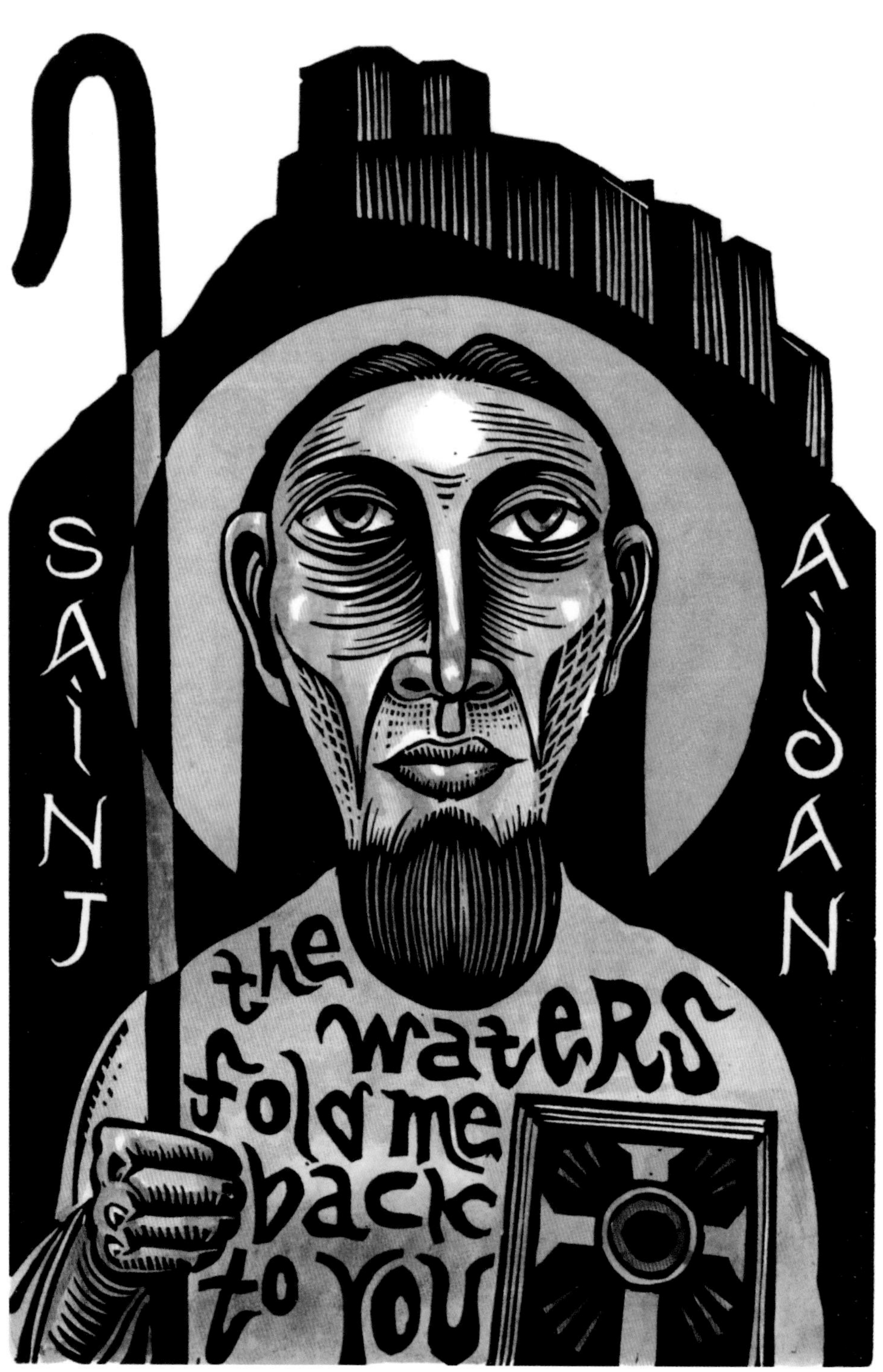
SAINT
AIDAN
the waters fold me back to you

Blessed are the peacemakers, for they will be called children of God.

—Matthew 5:9

Being a disciple of Christ isn't easy. The kingdom of God—sometimes referred to as the upside-down kingdom—defies the logic of the world, which maintains that if someone takes your eye, you take theirs! But Jesus challenges us to live in the kingdom of heaven *now*. "Do not resist an evil person," Jesus says, "If anyone slaps you on the right cheek, turn to them the other cheek also" (Matt 5:39).

Catholic journalist and peace activist Eileen Egan took this teaching about gospel nonviolence—a term she preferred over pacifism—to heart. A close friend of Mother Teresa and Dorothy Day, she likewise worked for healing and justice. Egan cofounded Pax Christi USA, an organization with a vision that "rejects war, preparation for war, every form of violence and domination, and personal and systemic racism."

Egan was once asked if people were justified in defending themselves. Wasn't it okay to harm others if they attacked you? She responded by saying, "Use the Eucharist as your defense." What an unusual tactic! Yet there might be truth here. As a shared meal, the Eucharist offers us God's grace and mercy. It absorbs us into the body of Christ, which takes the blows of hatred of those who attack. We become, in some way, cosufferers with Christ.

When Egan was eighty years old, she was attacked by a man on the streets of New York. Her hip was broken and seven ribs were fractured. In the aftermath, Egan chose not to testify against her attacker in court. She visited him while he was in jail, and she arranged for housing once he was released. "I look on my attacker as a human being," she reflected. "I don't want to push him further down. I'd rather raise him up."

No, following Jesus isn't easy. Yet by being conduits of his love, we can bring peace and healing to a weary world.

Prince of Peace, you offered your body and blood for me; you pleaded for the forgiveness of those who tortured and murdered you. Fill my heart with gospel nonviolence: with gentleness and love and peace that passes all understanding. Amen.

every human being is
sacred in the eyes of God
eileen egan

Give thanks in all circumstances. —1 THESSALONIANS 5:18

The Carmelite nun St. Thérèse of Lisieux lived a short life that burned with passion. The fuel? Gratitude! Thérèse discovered the secret early on: "Jesus does not ask for great deeds, but only for gratitude and self-surrender."

Thérèse's attitude is rather remarkable. Her mother died when she was just four years old. Pauline, her older sister and mother figure, moved out shortly thereafter, joining the convent at Lisieux. When Thérèse grew up and became a nun herself, she was plagued with physical illness, as well as extreme anxiety and religious guilt.

But thankfulness formed the bedrock of her spiritual growth. "With me, prayer is . . . a cry of gratitude and love, uttered equally in sorrow and in joy," she writes in her autobiography, *Story of a Soul*. It's easy to be thankful in seasons of blessing, but tending to this root in hard times is another story.

Giving thanks in all circumstances is possible when the goal is not happiness but Christlikeness. If happiness is our objective, then distractions and suffering will disappoint us every time. Neither love nor the cross are easy to bear. But we can learn to see trials and suffering as stepping stones to God's transformative intentions. It's not that we seek suffering, nor that God inflicts suffering on us; but in a world of light and darkness, we can expect a rough road. "You will have trouble," Jesus reminds us in John 16:33. "But take heart! I have overcome the world."

During difficult seasons, when the tide is moving out on one shore, we can turn around. Perhaps we can then observe the abundant wave approaching on the other. As the hymn goes, "Count your many blessings, name them one by one, count your many blessings, see what God has done."

We can aspire to a life steeped in gratitude. Were she still with us, Thérèse might remind us: all is a gift.

Gracious and Giving God, thank you for life: for the air I breathe and the water I drink. Thank you for all you've created that blesses and brings joy. Nurture within me a posture of gratitude. Amen.

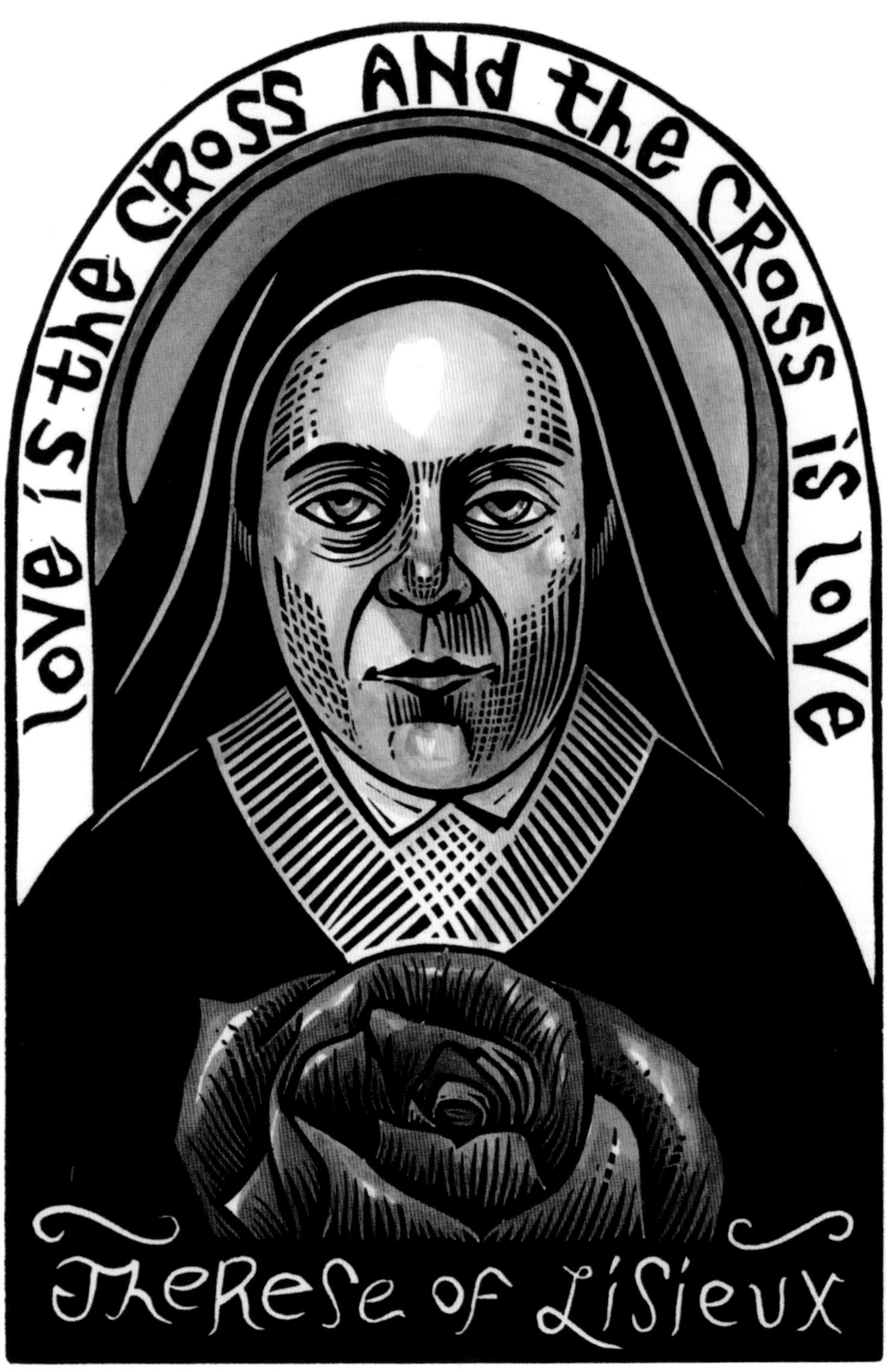
love is the CROSS AND the CROSS is love
THERESE OF LISIEUX

The Lord is good to all; he has compassion on all he has made.

—Psalm 145:9

Si'ahl (often known as "Seattle"), chief of the Suquamish and Duwamish tribes, was likely born at his mother's village, Stukw, in what we now know as Washington state. He watched as epidemic such as smallpox and measles, brought by the settlers, decimated his people and as traded goods and firearms began to change Indigenous cultures.

Chief Seattle came to faith in Christ late in life. He must have felt a strong kinship with this Middle Eastern man, Jesus. Jesus, after all, spoke of looking to the natural world to understand the Creator. He often spent entire evenings alone and with his brothers on the hills and mountains surrounding his native countryside, sleeping under the stars and living off the land. And he spoke of a way of life that undoubtedly the warring Seattle longed for: one of everlasting peace.

God had also spoken with Chief Seattle in the beautiful surroundings of what we now know as the American Northwest. He revered all that the Creator had made and provided for his people. He understood that humanity is "merely a strand in [the web of life]. Whatever he does to the web, he does to himself."

Chief Seattle spoke often of silence, simplicity, and stewardship. He talked of the brotherhood and sisterhood of the animal kingdom, the same life force that runs through our veins. Seattle stated, "This we know. The earth does not belong to man; man belongs to the earth. This we know. All things are connected like the blood which unites one family. All things are connected." His prophetic voice has an urgency for us today.

Chief Seattle's witness reminds us that God inhabits our very breath, and that all things need our care and compassion. We are all connected and intimately intertwined in the web of life by God's loving hand and good grace.

O Great Spirit, tenderly You walk beside us on the path called compassion and mercy. May harmony be the experience for us now, and for future generations to come. Amen.

TAKE NOTHING BUT MEMORIES, LEAVE NOTHING BUT FOOTPRINTS
CHIEF SEATTLE

MARTIN DE PORRES (1579–1639) Healing

Then Jesus, moved with compassion, stretched out His hand and touched him.

—Mark 1:41 NKJV

"Martin of Charity," the first Black saint of the Americas, grew up in Lima, Peru, in the late sixteenth century. His mother, a formerly enslaved woman, sent him to a Dominican Priory school, as she was unable to care for him due to financial difficulties. There he learned basic trades. His heart was tender toward God, and he desired to join the order.

Under Peruvian law, descendants of Africans and Native Americans were barred from becoming full-time members of religious orders. After Martin had served faithfully as a volunteer for eight years, the head prior bypassed the law and consented to his consecration.

Martin spent the last twenty-five years of his life working in the infirmary. What set Martin apart from the other men was his humility and kindness. He had the heartbeat of Christ within him. He once said, "Everything, even sweeping, scraping vegetables, weeding a garden and waiting on the sick could be a prayer if it were offered to God."

During his time in the infirmary, an epidemic broke out and infected sixty friars. They were placed in isolation, and Martin was the one who cared for their needs. Another time, an elderly man came to the monastery covered with ulcers. Martin slept elsewhere so that he could give the man his own bed. When reprimanded by a brother for doing this, Martin countered: "Compassion is preferable to cleanliness. Reflect that with a little soap I can easily clean my bed covers, but even with a torrent of tears I would never wash from my soul the stain that my harshness toward the unfortunate would create."

God worked mightily through Martin to bring about miraculous healing as well. While applying his medical knowledge for his patients' benefit, he admitted, "I cure them, but God heals them."

The Benedictine virtue of hospitality was not a chore for Martin but a privilege. He turned everything he did into a prayer.

Christ our Healer, help me make everything become a prayer. This is the state of attentive awareness I wish to live in—willing to serve, being used for your purposes and bringing healing wherever needed. Amen.

Martin
de Porres
everything could be a prayer, if it were offered to God

SADHU SUNDAR SINGH (1889–1929) Holiness

"Be holy, because I am holy." —1 PETER 1:16B

Sundar Singh's mother died when he was fourteen. Angry and grieving, he burned one of his holy books, the Bible. Yet he still sought relief from God for the pain and unrest he felt. Finally, Sundar determined that he would fast for three days. Then, if no answer came, he would place his head on the railroad track and wait for the morning train.

One-half hour before the train's arrival, a bright light entered his room. Initially he thought the room was on fire. Then, in the center of that light, Sundar saw Jesus. A voice spoke: "I have come to save you; you were praying to know the right way. Why do you not take it?" Sundar made that decision. He later recalled, "I experienced a peace that is unknown to the worldly."

The mercy of God filled him in such a way as to alter his life dramatically. "This was heaven itself," he would proclaim. From that day forth, he was willing to face all obstacles for Christ's sake, and he became a model of holiness.

Building upon his Sikh upbringing, Singh sojourned into the wilderness as a holy man—a sadhu—which had always been his mother's wish for him. "Seek peace of soul, and love God always," she said. "Someday, you must give yourself fully to the search; you must follow the way of the sadhu."

Singh's new perspective brought fresh insight to those who sought his advice. No longer was self-imposed suffering required, he taught; Christ had taken the world's pain and sins upon himself, giving us mercy, healing, and freedom.

O Holy One, Yesu, you've made me a holy vessel. I know you desire a deeper relationship with me. Birth this longing within my own soul too, so that I can say along with Sadhu Sundar Singh, "Where you are, there is heaven." Amen.

YOU ALONE DO I DESIRE AND WHERE YOU ARE THERE IS HEAVEN
SADHU SUNDAR SINGH

We also glory in our sufferings, because we know that suffering produces perseverance; perseverance, character; and character, hope.

—ROMANS 5:3–4

Argentine artist and peace activist Adolfo Pérez Esquivel paints a contemporary Christ in his *Stations of the Cross.* He shows Jesus as a dark-skinned Latin American man and offers new meanings for each station. For example, in station three, as Jesus is being crushed by the cross, the people are shown as being crushed by war. He depicts the death of priest Óscar Romero in the lower left while Jesus looks up at the gunman from a kneeling position.

In Esquivel's work, Jesus is clearly suffering with his people, as commentator David B. Gowler writes, as they experience "colonization, poverty, hunger, illiteracy, economic inequality, and other oppression including torture, imprisonment, and death."

Esquivel knows the brutality of militias and dictatorships. He left a university position to lead El Servicio de Paz y Justicia, an ecumenical organization that protects human rights in Latin America. A few years later, he was arrested and spent over a year in prison, where he was often tortured. His resolve to work for justice using peaceful means didn't waver, however, and upon his release, he was awarded the Nobel Peace Prize.

"We live in hope because, like St. Paul, we believe that love never dies," Esquivel stated in his 1980 Nobel acceptance speech. In Spanish, *esperar* can mean both "to wait" and "to hope." We wait and we hope in the possibilities of love to endure and to triumph over evil.

"Would that my voice could have the strength of voice of the humble, a voice that denounces injustice and proclaims hope in God and humanity," Esquivel said in his speech. "This is the hope of all human beings who long to live in harmony in common with all persons as brothers and sisters and as children of God."

Through tribulations, our hope is refined: a hope to heal and not harm, to bring peace and not war, to offer love and not hate.

O Sovereign One, you are our hope—the hope of glory! Give me hope when I risk losing it, and help me to open my hands and proclaim hope in you and in humanity. Amen.

WE cannot sow SEEDS
with clenched fists.
To sow we must open
our hands. ~ adolfo
ESQUIVEL

I was a stranger and you welcomed me. —MATTHEW 25:35 CEB

The Celtic saint Brigid founded an abbey in Kildare, just west of modern-day Dublin. The monastery included both monks and nuns. It became a great center of learning and piety, featuring metalworks and illuminated manuscripts. The abbey also became a place of hospitality. "I should welcome the poor to my feast, for they are God's children," Brigid states. "I should welcome the sick to my feast, for they are God's joy."

Stories and legends of Brigid's generosity abound. Her tender heart for the poor had compelled young Brigid to give away her father's belongings. In fact, she was giving away so many things that her father, fearing he might become impoverished, decided to marry her off. While he was in negotiations with a suitor, a person with leprosy passed by. Brigid offered him her father's jewel-studded sword. Her suitor, watching this unfold, was dismayed. Would she give away all his belongings as well? Brigid declared that she intended to marry no one on earth anyway, as she was the eternal spouse of Christ.

In another story, St. Brigid went to the king of Leinster to ask for land to build a convent. The king initially refused, but he relented when Brigid asked, "Will you give me as much land as my cloak will cover?" Knowing her cloak was small, he agreed. Four of her friends took the corners of the garment and began walking east, west, north, and south—and the cloak began stretching for miles! The king soon realized that God had blessed Brigid, and he granted her request for the land of Kildare.

Lines between legend and reality blur, but the truth of these stories is apparent: God is not short on treasures of mercy. "I would give all the wealth of Ireland away to serve the King of Heaven," Brigid says, "offering God's wealth to all."

Do we look at our possessions as ours or God's? Are we stagnate dams of envy or flowing rivers of God's hospitality?

God of the cattle on a thousand hills, sweet are your blessings that rain so generously upon us. Like St. Brigid, may we be hospitable to all, sharing your abundant gifts. Amen.

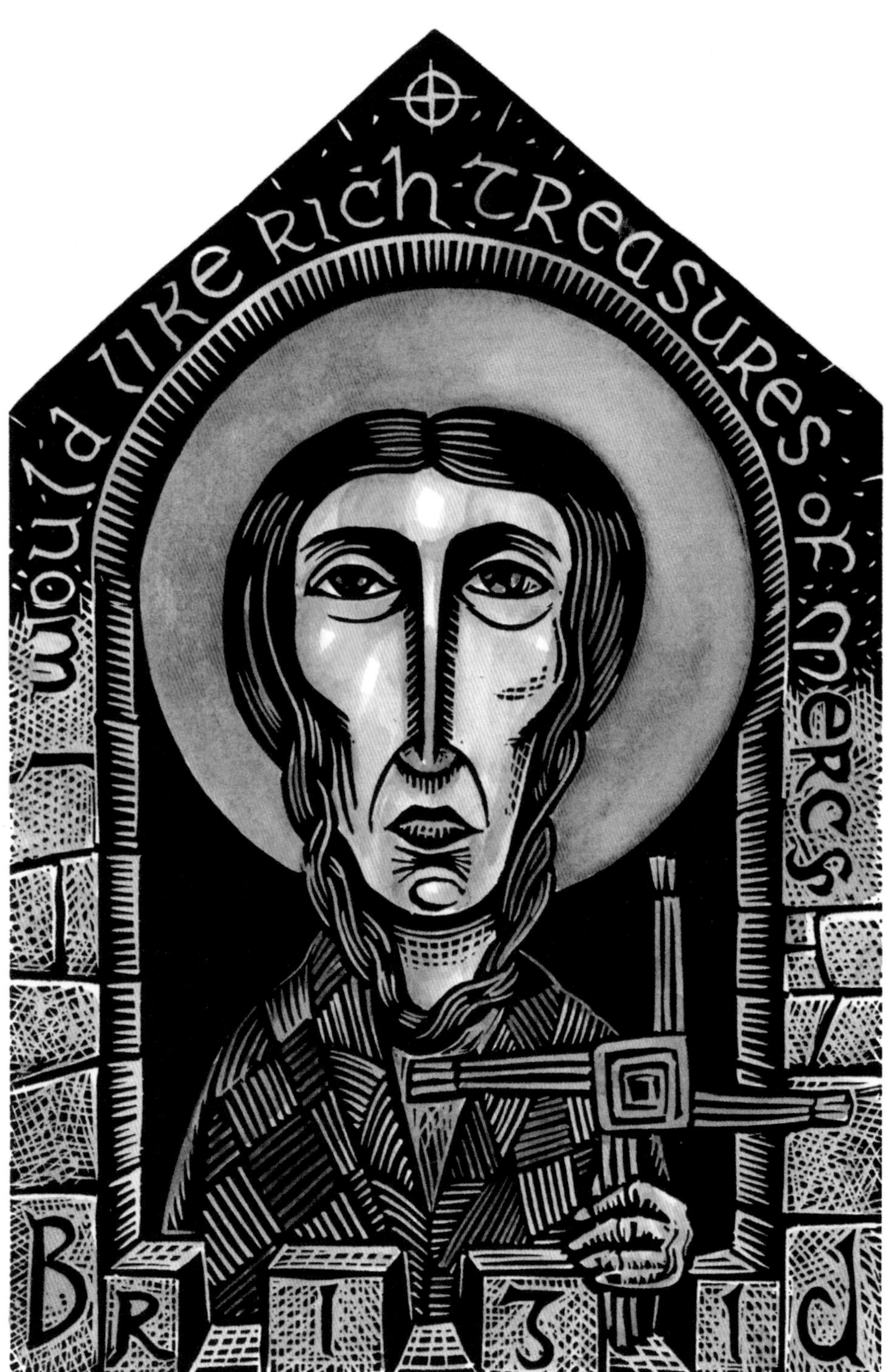
I would like rich treasures of mercy
BRIGID

Therefore, as God's chosen people, holy and dearly loved, clothe yourselves with . . . humility.

—COLOSSIANS 3:12

Benedictine spirituality grows out of the sixth-century monastic *Rule of Saint Benedict*. The seventy-three short chapters offer instruction on living life in a religious community. Benedict addresses the spiritual as well as the banal. The *Rule* includes instructions for the number of psalms to pray each day—and also how to care for the kitchen utensils! The rhythm and balance of life in Benedictine spirituality, known as *Ora et Labora* ("pray and work"), draw many to practice it.

One chapter of the *Rule* lists the order of psalms for daily prayer and at what hour to chant them. The recitation of these psalms has echoed throughout the ages. We could think of these prayers as the very heartbeat of the body of Christ.

St. Benedict is aware of the nature of this high calling. In the *Rule*, he precedes the instruction on prayer with his longest chapter on humility. Using the analogy of a ladder, he states, "We descend by exaltation and ascend by humility."

This upside-down kingdom is not only taught by Jesus but exhibited in his life. "The greatest among you will be your servant," Jesus says. So "take the lowest place," he suggests, as "those who humble themselves will be exalted" (Matt 23:11; Luke 14:10–11).

Trying to "achieve humility" is a catch-22, of course. Are truly humble people even aware of their own humility? Once humility is achieved, pride often comes rushing back . . . and humility vanishes.

Still, in a world in which we are surrounded by ladders of success, the humility we learn from St. Benedict is a refreshing virtue.

Humble Christ, give me the courage to be humble. Help me to serve others in all humility, with a purified heart and a tender soul. Amen.

ORA ET LABORA
BENEDICT

IGNATIUS OF LOYOLA (1491–1596) Imagination

I long to see you so that I may impart to you some spiritual gift to make you strong.
—Romans 1:11

Ignatius of Loyola lay bedridden and in severe pain, resulting from a broken leg, an injury received in the Battle of Pamplona. Unfortunately, his leg had to be broken again and reset after complications.

As months passed, in the boredom of his daily living, he turned to reading—the classics at first, and then an influential book, *Life of Christ*, by Ludolph of Saxony. During this time, Ignatius transitioned from a soldier of Spain to a soldier for Christ.

Unable to physically move, he began to do religious exercises in his mind. He harnessed his imagination to awaken himself to Bible stories. Much like we may find ourselves remembering scenes in movies, he found he could relive each passage of Scripture, placing himself in various roles—the disciple, the blind beggar, Mary Magdalene, or another person. Ignatius was allowing the Spirit to enter his spirit. This is called imaginative prayer.

Some Christians throughout history have been suspicious of the imagination. But Ignatius writes, "All the things in this world are gifts of God, created for us, to be the means by which we can come to know him better, love him more surely, and serve him more faithfully. As a result, we ought to appreciate and use these gifts of God insofar as they help us toward our goal of loving service and union with God."

Ignatius eventually wrote a month-long group of meditations known as the *Spiritual Exercises*. This method was instrumental in training the Jesuits (Society of Jesus), which Ignatius helped to found in 1540.

The *Spiritual Exercises* have become meaningful to many people in recent years, with updated versions by new authors for contemporary audiences. Together with Ignatius, we can imagine our way toward union with God. And God can use our imagination to communicate with us.

Christ of the mysteries, images stream from your being. By simply adjusting my dial to the right wavelength, I will be rich enough. Flow through my imagination with life-altering visions and dreams! Amen.

GiVE ME OnLY YOUR LOVE & GRACE, with THESE I WiLL BE RiCH EnOUGH!
EXERCITIA
SPIRITUALIA
IGNATIUS of LOYOLA

When Jesus saw this, he was indignant. He said to them, "Let the little children come to me, and do not hinder them, for the kingdom of God belongs to such as these."

—Mark 10:14

Óscar Romero's life took a turn when his friend and fellow priest Rutilio Grande was murdered. After that event, Romero became an indignant, outspoken critic of the military government of El Salvador and an advocate for the marginalized and impoverished. He became the archbishop of San Salvador. He also became a target when he started calling out Christians whose allegiance to their country and government superseded their loyalty to God.

Like Dr. Martin Luther King Jr. and Mahatma Gandhi, Romero sought to lead in the ways of Christ: peaceful work combined with righteous indignation. Romero stated, "We have never preached violence, except the violence of love, which left Christ nailed to a cross, the violence that we must each do to ourselves to overcome our selfishness and such cruel inequalities among us."

The way of the martyred Christ and of the cross would also be Romero's way. On March 24, 1980, while standing in front of the chapel altar at the Hospital de la Divina Providencia, having just given mass, Romero was gunned down. The shooter had stepped outside the passenger side of a car and fired through the open chapel door.

Romero's body lay at the feet of the statue of the crucified Christ just behind him. No one was convicted of Romero's murder, but a UN commission concluded that a Salvadoran politician and death squad leader had ordered it.

Romero's life, death, and solidarity with the poor echo that same voice of love that spoke from the cross. "Peace is the generous, tranquil contribution of all, to the good of all," Romero says, guiding us still today. "Peace is dynamism. Peace is generosity. It is right and it is duty."

Consuming Fire, make me an instrument of peace, to ease the burdens of others when I'm able, to do my small part. Amen.

Let us not tire
of Preaching Love; it
is the force that
will overcome
the world

HOWARD THURMAN (1899–1981) Inner Strength

But when he, the Spirit of truth, comes, he will guide you into all the truth.

—John 16:13

Born in the Deep South, Howard Thurman was the grandson of enslaved people and lived in the world of Jim Crow. The Ku Klux Klan was a power in the southern states, including the church, and most whites ignored the injustices their Black brothers and sisters faced.

Thurman was a man of peace and a key proponent in the civil rights movement. He developed a theology of radical nonviolence that influenced and shaped a generation of civil rights activists. He was an important mentor to many leaders, including Martin Luther King Jr. Dr. King was said to always carry a Bible and a copy of Thurman's *Jesus and the Disinherited* in his briefcase.

Once when young Howard was picking berries in a forest, a thunderstorm approached. In a panic, he began to run until he was lost. Then he recalled some wisdom from his grandmother, who was a formative influence in his life: stop, be still, look, and listen. As the storm lit up the evening sky, Thurman took this advice. He began to see recognizable landmarks. He followed them through the dark, each lightning strike illuminating the way.

Thurman learned a valuable lesson that day: what initially terrifies us can be overcome and bring us safely home. "Sometimes in the stillness of the quiet, if we listen," Thurman writes in *Meditations of the Heart*, "we can hear the whisper of the heart giving strength to weakness, courage to fear, hope to despair."

Like Thurman, we can develop inner strength and resolve: a reliance to hold fast to Christ through the storms of life.

Fire of Love, knowing you are my inner strength in times of trouble and fear is a blessing. I resolve to live according to your desires, despite the conflicts that I may face in this world. Amen.

OFTEN TO BE FREE MEANS THE ABILITY TO DEAL WITH ONE'S SITUATION SO AS NOT TO BE OVERCOME BY IT
HOWARD THURMAN

If it is possible, as far as it depends on you, live at peace with everyone.

—Romans 12:18

Racism is not new; it changes shape and form over time. How ingrained it is within so many contemporary churches—and how widespread it was among the supposedly holy men and women of the desert.

One of the stories found in the ancient *Apophthegmata Patrum* is this: "Another day when a council was being held in Scetis, the Fathers treated Moses with contempt in order to test him, saying, 'Why does this black man come among us?' When he heard this he kept silent. When the council was dismissed, they said to him, 'Abba, did that not grieve you at all?' He said to them, 'I was grieved, but I kept silence.'"

Abba Moses exhibited a Christ-like restraint that would have been foreign to him in his youth, when he would have just as soon inflicted vengeance on these desert fathers. But the years of intimate prayer had changed him. "Do not be at enmity with anybody, and do not foster enmity in your heart," he would later say; "do not hate one who is at enmity with his neighbor—and this is peace."

In another story, Moses is invited to judge a brother who has sinned. Although reluctant, he finally agrees and arrives with a partial basket of sand. The basket has many holes, and most of the sand has run out. When asked what this is all about, he replies, "My sins are running out behind me and I do not see them—yet here I have come today to pass judgment on the faults of another!"

Moses was martyred during an attack by marauders at the monastery in CE 405. He had been informed but chose not to run and refused to fight back. Unwilling to kill, he resigned himself to an inevitable outcome: what he saw as God's providence.

"Those who live by the sword will die by the sword," Abba Moses laments. At age seventy-five, he achieved a spirit of intimacy with God attained by very few.

Face of Love, the intimacy you offer is the intimacy I need: full of compassion and grace, nonjudgmental, quick to forgive and love, and resigned to peace. Amen.

GO, SIT IN YOUR CELL, AND YOUR CELL WILL TEACH YOU EVERYTHING
ABBA ✦ MOSES

Rejoice always; pray continually. —1 THESSALONIANS 5:16–17

The Way of a Pilgrim is a Christian classic about a man searching for the answer to St. Paul's plea to "pray without ceasing." In the allegory, a pilgrim travels throughout Ukraine, Russia, and Siberia. He visits monasteries and churches as he goes, making inquiries to spiritual directors: How is it possible to pray without stopping?

In time, he discovers a spiritual director who introduces him to the Jesus Prayer: "Sit down alone and in silence, lower your head, shut your eyes, breathe out gently, and imagine yourself looking into your own heart. Carry your mind, that is your thoughts, from your head to your heart. As you breathe out, say, 'Lord Jesus Christ, have mercy on me.'"

The pilgrim begins to repeat this prayer, eventually working his way up to saying it twelve thousand times throughout the day. By this point, his connection with God permeates all other aspects of his life.

The average person takes approximately 960 breaths per hour. In thirteen hours, one would have taken roughly 12,000 breaths. To pray without ceasing is to breathe in God and to maintain an attentive focus on the Divine at all times.

The beginning of the simple prayer, "Lord Jesus Christ," marks the authority of God. The second half, "Have mercy on me," acknowledges our need for forgiveness. The thirteenth-century spiritual writer Nikiphoros the Monk believes the Jesus Prayer "protects the intellect from distraction, renders it impregnable to diabolical acts, and every day increases its love and desire for God."

Whether the Jesus Prayer is said once, as Bartimaeus did in Mark 10:48, or thousands of times, humility is essential. To "pray without ceasing" is to make our life a prayer. For the pilgrim, it involved breathing the breath of God. The pilgrim confides, "After no great lapse of time I had the feeling that the prayer had, so to speak, by its own action passed from my lips to my heart."

Lord Jesus Christ, Son of God, have mercy on me, a sinner. Amen.

LORD JESUS CHRIST • SON OF GOD • HAVE MERCY ON ME A SINNER
THE PILGRIM

Take to heart what is written in it. —Revelation 1:3

Journaling is a tangible way of taking things to heart. Writing can help us know ourselves—and God. "I must put down on paper what I have become," writes Trappist monk Thomas Merton: "a complete and holy transparency: living, praying, and writing in light of the Holy Spirit."

Merton was born in France and died in Thailand, but he lived many years at the Abbey of Our Lady of Gethsemani in Kentucky. He came to fame through his early autobiography, *The Seven Storey Mountain*, which some hailed as a religious classic akin to St. Augustine's *Confessions*.

In the silence and solitude of Gethsemani, Merton wrote more than fifty books and two thousand poems. His journals, covering his monastic years from 1939 to 1968, give insight into Merton's spiritual life, activist leanings, interfaith dialogue, and candid observations. They were published as a seven-volume set.

Merton saw in his writings a possible pathway to sainthood. "To write is to think and to live," he says, "and also, in some degree, even to pray."

Merton's honesty made him vulnerable, and it was a means to "become true." Writing down his thoughts in his hermitage, a place on the outskirts of the property to which he would occasionally retreat, became a spiritual exercise. It was a means to wrestle with God and himself, to question his theology, and to engage with nature. One writer says it was a way to "[live] out more consciously the meaning of his life."

There are no rules for how to journal. Entries can be short or long, with subjects that range from the mundane to the transcendent. A spiritual journal becomes a tool to experience God. It can bring clarity and release burdens.

Living Word, transparency is at the heart of a healthy relationship. With you as my advocate, I can search my soul and put my thoughts into written words—honest and true. Help me, as Merton suggests, to penetrate deeper into the things I know to be true. Amen.

IN SILENCE GOD CEASES TO BE AN OBJECT & BECOMES AN EXPERIENCE
THOMAS MERTON

C. S. LEWIS (1898–1963) Joy

May the God of hope fill you with all joy and peace as you trust in him.

—Romans 15:13

In 1939, Clive Staples Lewis got an idea for a children's book. During World War II, children had been evacuated from England's major cities, and Lewis offered some of them a home. One child was fascinated by his wardrobe, believing an exit must be on the other side. With that, the seed for *The Lion, the Witch, and the Wardrobe* was planted.

Lewis eventually wrote seven children's books in the Chronicles of Narnia series, from 1950 to 1956. The atheist-turned-Christian also wrote books defending the faith or addressing theological concepts: *Mere Christianity*, *The Screwtape Letters*, and *The Problem of Pain*, being just a few.

When Lewis came to faith in Christ, he discovered an unspeakable inner joy. In fact, the memoir of his conversion is titled *Surprised by Joy*. And this joy went deeper than happiness; it wasn't dependent on his circumstances or desires. "If you want joy," Lewis observes, "you must get close to, or even into, the thing that has them." He argued that the same free will God gave us that makes evil possible also allows for any "joy worth having."

Joy—along with love, peace, patience, and other attributes—is considered one of the nine fruits of the Spirit in Galatians. It comes from the Greek word *chara*, which describes a feeling of inner gladness, delight, or rejoicing based on spiritual realities.

If God surprised the former atheist with inner joy, then the fantastical landscape of the childhood imagination provided a playground for that joy. Lewis's stories—replete with talking animals, magic rings, and the beloved lion Aslan—have brought wonder and joy to the lives of many generations. The joy Lewis had received so many years prior he generously gave back to children and the young of heart.

Lion of Judah, fill me with an infectious joy that bubbles over and affects those around me. In the midst of all the evil and suffering in this world, sustain, uplift, and encourage me with your joy. Amen.

O THOU FAIR SILENCE, FALL, AND SET ME FREE
C. S. LEWIS

And surely I am with you always, to the very end of the age.

—Matthew 28:20

When her own world came to an end, Mamie Till made a nation look at its own brutality. With God as her strength, the young woman from Chicago became a force for justice.

Nothing could have prepared her for the lynching of her son, Emmett. Nor was she ready for the injustices in the aftermath that followed. Through the passing years, one thing was clear: Mamie Till knew what it meant to lose a son for the greater good of others.

The casket containing his body was shipped back to Chicago from Mississippi, at a cost to her of nearly a one-year salary. She made the decision to have an open-casket funeral so that others could witness the brutality done to her son. Mamie Till showed America to itself in the unrecognizable body of her son.

The murder and ensuing injustices became a rallying cry for racial equality in all states: a civil rights turning point. The acquittal of the two men who committed the crime by an all-white male jury on November 9, 1955, was definitely on the mind of Rosa Parks a month later, when she refused to give up her seat. "With each day, I give thanks for the blessings of life—the blessings of another day and the chance to do something with it. Something good. Something significant. Something helpful. No matter how small it might seem. I want to keep making a difference," Till reflects.

Mamie Till would have given up everything to have her son back. But she made the best of it. As a teacher and an advocate for children in poverty, Till will later say, "I have left something of myself in all the children I have touched." And that would include the son she got to love for fourteen short years.

O God, comfort those who have lost loved ones to injustice. We are grateful for another day: a day to make the correct decision; to do something helpful and kind, no matter how small; to seek justice for those who have none. Amen.

I have taken one from you, but I will give you thousands
God told me
mamie TiLL

The Lord God took the man and put him in the Garden of Eden to work it and take care of it.

—Genesis 2:15

Black Elk, of the Oglala Lakota people, knew a deep intimacy with God's creation. His understanding of God—Wakan-Tanka—was not only as Creator but also Provider and Sustainer. God is closer than our heartbeat: closer than our very breath. Black Elk lived within the spirit of *mitakuye oyasin,* which means something like "I am connected to all creation" and "All beings are my relatives."

The Lakota perceived humans' connections with nature and the animal kingdom as God's gifts. With sorrow, they expressed their gratitude to both the Creator and the creatures that provided and sustained them with food, shelter, and clothing. With reverence, they prohibited killing for sport.

This tenderness is heard in Black Elk's plea, taken from a vision he had: "The Earth is your Grandmother and Mother, and She is sacred. Every step that is taken upon Her should be as a prayer."

Black Elk came to see Jesus as a Lakota at heart—one who exhibited all the values required by Wakan-Tanka. "I have come to the conclusion that this Jesus was an Indian," one Lakota elder has said. "He was opposed to material acquisition and to great possessions. He was inclined to peace. He was as unpractical as any Indian and set no price upon his labor of love."

Black Elk's spiritual wisdom is sorely needed today. What if all beings are kin and every step upon the Earth is a prayer?

O Great Spirit of all nations and tribes, I acknowledge you as the Creator of all that is. I listen for your voice in the cool breeze, and sense your presence in the fragrance of the flower. Help me to walk tenderly on this earth, peacefully, and in kinship with all people, with gratitude and praise. Amen.

LET EVERY STEP YOU TAKE UPON THE EARTH BE AS A PRAYER
BLACK ELK

Pour out your heart like water in the presence of the Lord. Lift up your hands to him for the lives of your children, who faint from hunger at every street corner.

—LAMENTATIONS 2:19

Lament is a foreign concept for churches in the West. Many Christians learn to deny feelings, including sadness, that don't seem to fit Sunday mornings of praise and worship. But the world is full of suffering that warrants our sorrow.

The psalms of lament are more plentiful than any other type of prayer in the Psalter. They follow similar outlines: addressing God, expressing the psalmist's complaint, asking for God's intervention, and trusting God's sovereignty.

The Psalms were the ascetic monk John Cassian's daily bread. He honed his virtues in the Egyptian desert under the tutelage of Evagrius Ponticus, Abba Moses, and Abba Isaac. And he helped to bring the wisdom of Egyptian monasticism to the West.

The "gift of tears" was a trait the early desert monks described. Sorrow and regret for one's sins, they maintained, could lead to repentance and new beginnings. In biblical times, people fasted, put on sackcloth, shaved their heads, and poured dirt over themselves. We find several examples in the Old Testament of all the Hebrew people doing this together. These acts of lament were an outward demonstration of an inward devastation.

In his writing, John Cassian seeks out Abba Isaac for his instruction on compunction: sorrow over his sins. Cassian records a variety of "convictions which spring from tears." The depth of these feelings is enough to alter one's direction in life. While many convictions are about individual sins, Abba Isaac instructs, "There is too another kind of tears, which are caused not by knowledge of one's self but by the hardness and sins of others."

As the body of Christ, we hurt when others hurt. Lament can involve feeling the devastation of others. "Mourn with those who mourn," writes St. Paul (Rom 12:15). Those given the "gift of tears" show us that lament is a vital part of the life of faith.

Weeping Christ, hasten to help me. May my tears refresh the soil of repentance and concern for others. Bring forth blossoms of healing and regeneration. Amen.

GOD, come to my assistance LORD, make haste to help me
JOHN CASSIAN

Unless a kernel of wheat falls to the ground and dies, it remains only a single seed. But if it dies, it produces many seeds.

—JOHN 12:24

Martin Luther King Jr. lived out Jesus's teachings on a grand scale: turning the other cheek to his oppressor and loving in the face of hate. "We've got to revolt in such a way that after revolt is over we can live with people as their brothers and their sisters," he preaches. "Our aim must never be to defeat them or humiliate them." Getting others to agree with him and live out Christ's teachings, knowing they would be in harm's way, was nothing short of miraculous.

As a leader, King lived his conviction. "Once, in Montgomery, I saw a man strike him, and he did not grimace or show anger," his spiritual brother and comrade Rev. Fred Shuttlesworth once reflected. "Instead, he turned a melancholy, forgiving face to his young white assailant, and refused to prosecute." King knew that to bring about such a seismic shift of equality was beyond his control. True justice would only find completion through God's divine guidance.

With the heat of hatred breathing down his neck, surely Brother Martin knew his days were limited. In his final speech, he prophesies that God "allowed me to go up to the mountain. And I've looked over, and I've seen the Promised Land. I may not get there with you." But in that final speech, he is clear: "I just want to do God's will."

The hallowed ground of the Lorraine Motel, where Rev. Martin Luther King Jr. took his final breath, is now home to the National Civil Rights Museum. There's an eerie silence and somber tone as people come and go. The man who died there could say, "Follow me, as I follow Christ," just like St. Paul did.

O Most High, grant that I address the injustices in this world with a Christ-like spirit of love: honestly, respectfully, and peacefully. Raise up humble and sensitive leaders of moral character who can bring us to the mountain of hope! Amen.

darkness cannot
drive out darkness
only light can
do that

My heart meditated and my spirit asked. —Psalm 77:6b

We can encounter Scripture in so many fruitful ways. In his sixth-century monastic *Rule*, St. Benedict instructed his monks to do "prayerful reading." Centuries later, Guigo II, a Carthusian monk, would construct a metaphorical four-rung ladder to define the process known as *lectio divina*, Latin for "divine reading." If studying Scripture informs our theology, and devotional reading inspires our soul, *lectio divina* transforms our spirits.

The four stages for *lectio divina*, what Guigo calls "spiritual work," consist of *lectio* (reading), *meditatio* (meditation), *oratio* (prayer), and *contemplatio* (contemplation).

Reading. We choose a text from Scripture and slowly read it until something catches our attention. Writing down this passage, sentence, or word can be beneficial, helping us slow down.

Meditation. We reread the text while meditating on specific words. This isn't a Bible study in which we look up definitions of those words; we encounter them with love. "Chewing the cud" is how Thomas Cranmer describes this stage. In his book *Sacred Reading*, Michael Casey suggests, "Dialogue with the text as though it were a person, asking it questions and listening for responses within us."

Prayer. We can pray about the text or pray with the text. In using lectio with the Psalms, I have often been prompted to expand on the psalmist's prayer, making it my own. Our responses will vary based on our current situation. Worship, thanksgiving, intercession, and repentance are all possible responses. It is the word that's "living and active" within us.

Contemplation. A time of silence is now needed. During contemplatio we rest, and all activity ceases. During this stage, as Basil Pennington writes in his book on sacred reading, "We abide with God within his temple."

Some say that lectio is less about us reading the text and more about allowing the text to read *us*. Love brings us to this place, where we can simply enjoy being in God's presence.

Light, my light, I wish to dwell in your presence: to experience you afresh. Teach me your ways, guide me in understanding, renew me again. Amen.

LECTIO · MEDITATIO · ORATIO · CONTEMPLATIO
GUIGO II

MAXIMILIAN KOLBE (1894–1941) Love

Greater love has no one than this: to lay down one's life for one's friends.

—John 15:13

The loud screeching of the train brakes carrying the condemned into Auschwitz gave way to the orders of the commander. The prisoners, clad in thin, torn, striped uniforms, fell quickly in line. The commander was going to call out ten men by number to be starved to death as retribution after three inmates were assumed to have escaped.

One of the prisoners was a Polish man named Maximilian Kolbe, a Franciscan priest arrested for harboring Jews. During the war, the friary acted as a makeshift hospital, print shop, radio station, and homeless shelter. It was not unusual to see Kolbe give away his small rations to someone in need, always trusting in God's providence.

But this day would demand of him a far greater sacrifice. One of the prisoners chosen, Franciszek Gajowniczek, burst into tears upon hearing his number called. His hopes of ever seeing his wife and two young children again vanished.

At that moment, Kolbe did the unthinkable. He stepped forward to offer his life in exchange for Gajowniczek's. Surprisingly, his request was granted. Two weeks passed, with the prisoners locked in a room with no food. When the jailer came to remove the dead bodies, he discovered Kolbe, praying in the corner and consoling three others who were still alive. They all were administered a deadly shot of carbolic acid.

Gajowniczek survived Auschwitz. "I could only thank him with my eyes," he laments later. "I was stunned and could hardly grasp what was going on. The immensity of it: I, the condemned, am to live and someone else willingly and voluntarily offers his life for me—a stranger. Is this some dream?"

"A single act of love makes the soul return to life," Kolbe says. A single act of sacrificial love changes everything for those who bear witness to this love.

Man of Sorrows, Sacrificing Shepherd, you who lay down your life for the sheep: with gratitude and praise I thank you with all my heart, with all my life, and with all my spirit for giving fully of yourself, and for showing us what real love is! Amen.

for Jesus Christ I am
Prepared to Suffer
16670
MAXIMILIAN KOLBE

Then you will be handed over to be persecuted and put to death, and you will be hated by all nations because of me.

—Matthew 24:9

Sitting in the hot afternoon sun, the bloodthirsty crowd in Carthage was growing impatient. Having tasted the gory deaths of Saturninus, Revocatus, and Saturus by wild beasts, they now awaited the main course.

Two Christian women—Perpetua, a young mother, and Felicitas, her servant—were to be put to death, and the crowd desired to make examples of them. They'd show them what happens when you're not loyal to the state. Stripped and clothed with nets, Perpetua and Felicitas were led into the arena to face the wild bull.

The courage of Perpetua and Felicitas, and the details of their imprisonment and death, are recorded in Perpetua's diary, which was finished by a friend. A few things become apparent: Perpetua loved her newborn son and was concerned for his well-being. That love was matched only by her passion for Christ. And she cared deeply for Felicitas. It's written that when "she saw Felicitas crushed, she approached, gave her her hand, and lifted her up. And both of them stood together."

Martyrdom—relinquishing one's life to the point of death for the sake of a person or cause—is a strange concept for those accustomed to religious freedom. Yet many governments persecute Christians for their faith. How is it that some people of faith choose to be loyal to the truth all the way to death?

Jesus's resurrection produced a radical shift. Immediately after his death, his disciples were fearful, huddling behind locked doors. Yet three days later they were emboldened. All of them were now willing to come out of hiding and die a martyr's death.

We are indebted to Perpetua and Felicitas, the men who died with them that day, and to all those who have been so loyal to Christ. Their lives and deaths pose a question to all of us: What might loyalty to Christ require?

Light to the nations, my faith is encouraged by those we call martyrs. Shape my allegiances and affections, and make me willing to stand fast for you and those you love. Amen.

STAND FAST IN THE FAITH &
PERPETUA
FELICITAS
LOVE ONE ANOTHER

Show me your faith without deeds, and I will show you my faith by my deeds.

—JAMES 2:18

Along with Nelson Mandela, Desmond Tutu began the laborious process of dismantling apartheid and introducing democracy in South Africa. Tutu spoke out against the injustices of those marginalized by white supremacy. He also sought no revenge against the perpetrators. "When I forgive . . . I open the door of opportunity to you to make a new beginning," he states. Like Gandhi and Martin Luther King Jr., Tutu discovered in the teachings of Jesus a better way, not just personally but for society.

A man of prayer and study, Tutu practiced what he preached. His contemplative life aligned with his social activism. While leading the South African Council of Churches (SACC)—one of the few Christian institutions in South Africa in which Black people had the majority representation—he incorporated a regime of daily staff prayers, regular Bible study, a monthly Eucharist, and silent retreats. As a Spirit-led force, he hoped that the SACC would one day advance human rights.

In 1985, Tutu became the bishop of Johannesburg. From this position of power, he appealed to foreign governments to apply economic pressure on South Africa. "I have no hope of real change from our government unless they are forced," Tutu confessed. "I call on the international community to apply punitive sanctions against this government to help us establish a new South Africa—non-racial, democratic, participatory, and just. This is a non-violent strategy to help us do so."

Tutu's tireless work of speaking out against injustice, organizing strikes, and leading peaceful protests paid off. By the early 1990s, apartheid had been dismantled.

Archbishop Tutu could have become a voice for vengeance and violence; instead, he became a leader of mercy. "Do your little bit of good where you are," Tutu encourages us; "it's those little bits of good put together that overwhelm the world."

O Merciful One, I see you in the eyes of the stranger but often show no mercy. Widen my heart to embrace those who are different than me, and in so loving them, love you. Amen.

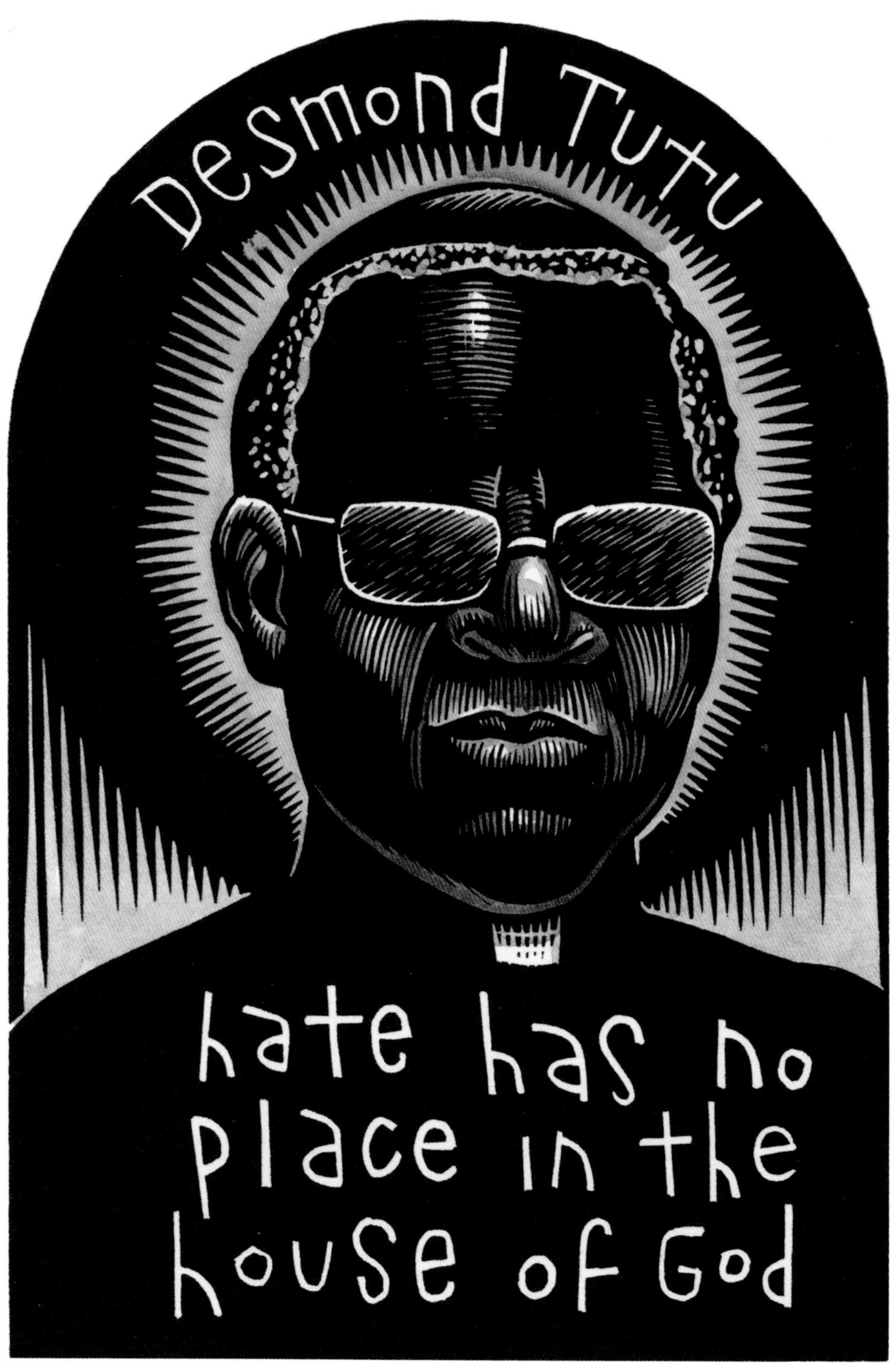
Desmond Tutu
hate has no
place in the
house of God

This is my body, which is for you; do this in remembrance of me.

—1 Corinthians 11:24

The voyage of St. Brendan is recorded in the early ninth-century writing *Navigatio Brendani.* The journey retold in this Irish epic is replete with fantastical sea creatures, mysterious islands, colorful characters, and wondrous encounters. As Brendan and his men search for the Island of paradise, they find islands covered with birds that talk and sheep that are bigger than cattle. The book is allegory and odyssey. We find in its pages the ultimate *peregrinus*—the risk-taking traveler—searching for the promises of God.

In one story, Brendan and his men encounter an unusual island. The brothers spend the evening in worship and sing mass in the morning, while Brendan remains in the boat. When they start a fire to cook breakfast, the island begins to move. They rush to the ship, terrified. Safely aboard the boat, they realize the island was not an island after all; they are being stranded on the back of a whale.

This encounter takes place on Maundy Thursday, but it would become an annual ritual. "Easter you will celebrate on the back of the whale," the bird of paradise spoke to them, "until the seven years of your pilgrimage are over."

The back of the whale becomes a place of comfort, not fear. Just as Jonah survived in the belly of a whale for three days, so Christ overcame the grave after three days. They feast on the back of the beast with the bread and wine of Christ's loving sacrifice—the holy meal. The great mystery of grace.

Each of us has our own fantastic—and maybe fantastical!—story to tell. Like Brendan and his companions, we can partake in the Eucharist. We can marvel at all we don't understand, and we can savor the mysteries of our faith.

Captain of my soul, as I travel and encounter mysteries unknown, I shall not be fearful but look to You. With St. Brendan, I pray, "O King of mysteries . . . I throw myself wholly upon you . . . Shall I take my tiny boat across the wide sparkling ocean? O Christ, will you help me on the wild waves?" Amen.

CHRIST OF THE MYSTER-IES
I TRUST YOU
St. Brendan

I pray . . . that all of them may be one, Father, just as you are in me and I am in you. May they also be in us so that the world may believe that you sent me.

—John 17:20–21

The journey of the mystic is a journey toward union with God. Since God is eternal, this is a never-ending process. One can always move toward greater love and intimacy.

The sixteenth-century Carmelite nun St. Teresa writes about this spiritual path in her book *The Interior Castle*. Unlike the metaphor of a ladder that many other mystical writers use, Teresa's way is more of a labyrinth. It circles ever inward, as if attracted by a giant magnet. Her vision of the soul as a clear crystal becomes the garden where the Divine wishes to dwell. "Christ has no body now but mine," Teresa states. "He prays in me, works in me, looks through my eyes, speaks through my words, works through my hands, walks with my feet and loves with me here."

As we enter the interior castle, we meander through various rooms, defining God and humanity, prayer and penance, and love beyond reason. Midway, we stop in the prayer of quiet. At this stage, Teresa encourages us to stop striving through human efforts of prayer and find the source of this spring—from "doing" to "being."

The final three stages of Teresa's spiritual path become more vague and less defined: growing union and resisting temptation; wounds of love; and finally, spiritual marriage.

We are each unique individuals, and our spiritual journeys will undoubtedly reflect our own ways of being. Yet Teresa's longing for oneness with the Godhead (John 17:21) captures many of our experiences through spiritual formation.

We desire union with an eternal Christ, and we invite him to pray in us, work in us, and love through us. God indeed suffices.

O Beloved of my heart, guide me as I walk this labyrinth; it seems to lead only to you. Help me respond to your grace: when to move, when to be still. I pray in agreement with Teresa, "May your will be done, in time and in eternity by me, in me, and through me." Amen.

LET NOTHING FRIGHTEN YOU, ALL THINGS ARE PASSING ... GOD SUFFICES
TERESA OF AVILA

Then he said to them all: "Whoever wants to be my disciple must deny themselves and take up their cross daily and follow me."

—Luke 9:23

Simon was from Cyrene, more than one thousand miles from Jerusalem, on the northern tip of Africa. He might have arrived by land, or more likely by boat, sailing eastward across the Mediterranean Sea. We don't know why he was in Jerusalem, but we do know his life was about to take a sudden turn.

As Simon enters the city, he comes upon a crowd and makes his way to the center to see what all the commotion is about. He sees a bloodied man, down on his knees, desperately trying to get back up to lift a heavy cross. Mark writes, "They compelled a certain man, Simon a Cyrenian, the father of Alexander and Rufus, as he was coming out of the country and passing by, to bear His cross." The Greek word ἀγγαρεύουσιν has been interpreted as "forced," "compelled," "seized." He couldn't say no to the heavily armed Roman guard.

What are Simon's thoughts as he adjusts the cross onto his own shoulders and gets pelted with rocks and spittle? Does Jesus give him a kind glance or whisper a weak thank you?

A couple years earlier, Jesus had taught his followers that if an enemy forces you to go with him one mile, go with him two. Jesus actually gives his followers the upper hand in this scenario; we have the last say-so. Your evil intention cannot outdo my good one. Your injustice cannot take away my dignity.

There may come a time when we will be placed in a position like Simon was. What a horrible honor. What a terrible but beautiful accompaniment. May we be as obedient as he was.

Grant me, O Radiant One, a willing spirit and an obedient heart, so that I may be your instrument for change here on earth. Empower me with your Spirit to go the extra mile not grudgingly, but with kindness and generosity. Amen.

HIM THEY COMPELLED TO BEAR HIS CROSS
ST SIMON OF CYRENE

Love the Lord your God with all your heart. —Luke 10:27

Abba Joseph was a hermit living on the fringe of a monastic community in North Africa. Novices would seek him out for wisdom. With his balanced good humor, hospitality, and insight, he'd present them with a short response tailored to their needs.

Abba Lot was one of his disciples. Like Joseph, he observed the spiritual disciplines. Approaching his teacher, he asks, "Abba, as far as I can I say my little office, I fast a little, I pray and meditate, I live in peace and as far as I can, I purify my thoughts. What else can I do?"

The old man rises to his feet and stretches "his hands towards heaven. His fingers became like ten lamps of fire and he said to him, 'If you will, you can become all flame.'"

You need to be consumed with a passionate love for God, Abba Joseph suggests. The spiritual life is not a set of rules but an ardent love affair! If rules take the place of love, they're useless. If I do "not have love, I gain nothing," St. Paul wrote (1 Corinthians 13:3).

The spiritual walk is not a short-term infatuation. It is a committed loyalty and long desire. It moves us away from a narcissistic love of God for our own sake to loving God for God's sake. We cannot quantify this love. We can only let it blaze.

What if we could become love itself, like God? What if we could love God and our neighbor and ourselves? What if we were to become all flame?

Spirit of Fire, ignite a flame within my heart! May my life burn with passion for you and for doing your will. Take my little light and join that flame with others. Consume us in your everlasting love. Amen.

IF YOU WOULD, YOU COULD BECOME ALL FLAME
ABBA JOSEPH

Please him in every way . . . being strengthened with all power . . . so that you may have great endurance and patience.

—Colossians 1:10–11

Fertilizing the ground of the heart for love to grow was paramount for the early church fathers and mothers. Desert monastics sought two essential virtues: humility and patience.

St. Basil, one of the three Cappadocian fathers (along with Gregory of Nyssa and Gregory of Nazianzus), lived in what is modern-day Turkey. Given the title *Great* in the Eastern Orthodox Church, he is considered a saint within both Eastern and Western Christian traditions. He admonishes us to "bear with patience everything the world throws at us." It is during these difficult times "that we are most in the mind of God."

While some people are predisposed toward patience, others are not. But patience can be cultivated. If we are easily frustrated or prone to outbursts of anger, God seems to have a way of placing us in situations that hone this skill. Once we realize the world doesn't revolve around us but around God, we can step back and learn to trust.

St. Paul instructs young Timothy to "correct, rebuke and encourage—with great patience and careful instruction" (2 Tim 4:2). By relinquishing our control—or what we *perceive* as our control—to God, we can learn to love without manipulating others. Patience, one of the fruits of the Spirit, grows in us through each trial we pass.

We don't know all the trials St. Basil faced. We do know that as bishop of Caesarea, he preached to large congregations and also built a hospital, hospice, and home for those who lived in poverty. "There is still time for endurance, time for patience, time for healing, time for change," Basil encourages us. "Have you slipped? Rise up. Have you sinned? Cease."

We do not learn the mind of God overnight. Patience doesn't come in a day—or even a lifetime. But in the life we live now, we can live by the Spirit and find the quiet harbor to which God steers us.

O Merciful Presence, I relinquish to you my frustrations and impatient ways when things don't go according to my desires. Help me to make your plans my plans. Amen.

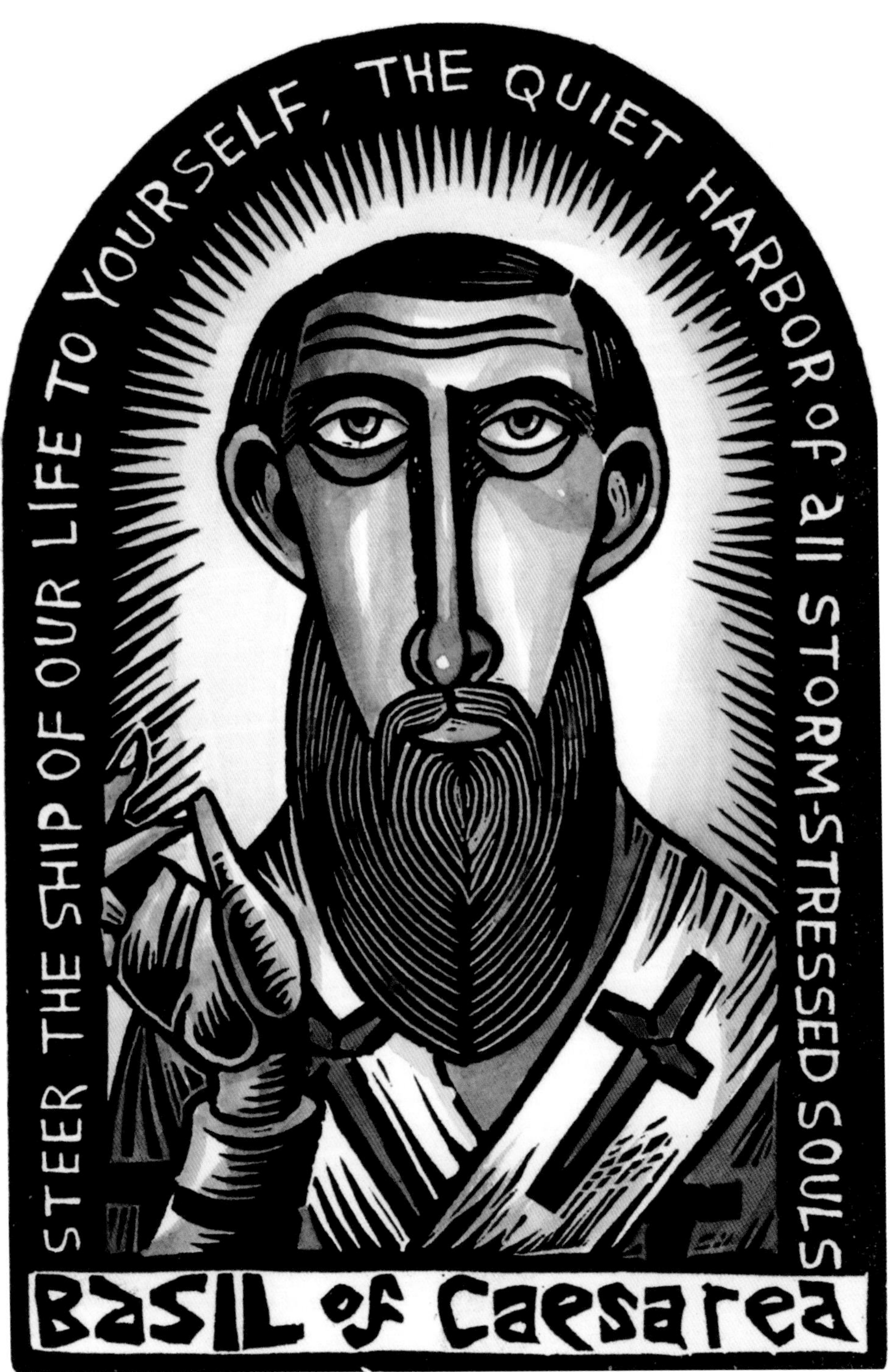
STEER THE SHIP OF OUR LIFE TO YOURSELF, THE QUIET HARBOR OF ALL STORM-STRESSED SOULS
BASIL OF CAESAREA

Be strong and courageous. Do not be afraid or terrified because of them, for the Lord your God goes with you; he will never leave you nor forsake you.

—Deuteronomy 31:6

The evening was hot and humid as the small group made their way through the thicket and along the riverbank. The full moon illuminated the landscape, allowing them to find their footing. Harriet stopped abruptly and grabbed her forehead. Another excruciating headache was coming on, and a seizure that brought her to her knees. The others stood motionless as the dogs in the distance grew louder.

When the convulsing subsided, Harriet composed herself and pointed. "This way," she whispered, "the Lord done told me so." They followed her into the cool water, up to their necks at times, among the reeds. She motioned with her hand for them to hold their breaths as she disappeared beneath the river current. "It wasn't me, it was the Lord," Tubman later said. She told the Lord, "'I don't know where to go or what to do, but I expect You to lead me,' and he always did."

Harriet Tubman, born into slavery, escaped in 1849. Her first journey into freedom was like a born-again experience: "I looked at my hands to see if I was the same person now I was free," she said. "There was such glory over everything. The sun came up like gold through the trees, and I felt like I was in heaven."

Most people would have been content to stay in "heaven." Not Harriet. With a bounty on her head, Tubman risked her life thirteen more times, traversing from Pennsylvania to Maryland and back again, always following that north star. With perseverance, she led some seventy enslaved people to freedom. Later, as a scout for the Union army, she led an action that liberated seven hundred more.

Harriet Tubman's perseverance, shown through her repeated journeys to emancipate others is how she came to be called the Moses of her people.

Christ, our North Star, thank you for Harriet: for her bravery, courage, and living example of what it means to persevere. I expect you to lead me. Empower me and all people in the quest for liberation. Amen.

LORD, I TRUST YOU. I EXPECT YOU TO LEAD ME
HARRIET TUBMAN

Go in peace. Your journey has the Lord's approval. —JUDGES 18:6

The sixth-century monastic Celtic saint Columba, also known as Colmcille, was a poet, scholar, and perhaps a painter. Some have attributed parts of the *Book of Kells* to him. He founded monasteries and educated disciples.

Following a copyright infringement dispute over an illuminated psalter he had copied, violence between various clans erupted. Despondent over the carnage, Columba climbed into his coracle, a small, rudderless boat made of animal skins. He set off into the water, allowing the breath of God to direct him.

It was not unusual for Celtic monks to relinquish control to the divine will as they took to the high seas. *Peregrinatio pro Christo*, which means "pilgrimage for Christ," was often used to describe the wanderings of such adventurers. Columba's prayer captures his confidence in this undertaking: "Alone with none but thee, my God, I journey on my way. What need I fear, when thou art near, O King of night and day? More safe am I within thy hand, than if a host didst round me stand."

After many days adrift, the boat washed ashore on the rocky Isle of Iona, off the southwestern tip of Scotland. Iona would become a monastic settlement known as a "thin place": a portal between heaven and earth, a liminal space where one could hear angels' whispers. Like Jerusalem or Santiago de Compostela in Spain, the sacred island is now a major pilgrimage destination, known as a place of prayer, worship, and the word. People flock to its shores. Some come hoping to find direction or healing. Some wish for a spiritual encounter, while others simply want to explore the historical ruins and enjoy the beauty.

Pilgrimage can reanimate a faith that has become dull and routine. Like Columba, we are all wanderers. Traveling to thin places—or finding those places right where we live—may very well open up sacred encounters. No matter where we go, God will be a bright flame and a guiding star.

God, my Coracle, as I journey through life, taking risks and living by faith, I pray with Columba that "the fire of your love burns brightly and steadfastly in my heart like the golden light within the sanctuary lamp." Amen.

BE THOU A BRIGHT FLAME BEFORE ME; BE THOU A GUIDING STAR ABOVE ME;
COLUMBA of IONA

JACOPONE DA TODI (1230–1306) Praise

Praise the Lord. Praise God in his sanctuary; praise him in his mighty heavens.
—Psalm 150:1

Jacopone da Todi was madly in love with his new bride. A lawyer born to a wealthy family in northern Italy, he was as imperious and greedy as his new wife was humble and kind. But his dreams of building a future with her came crashing down when she died in a freak accident.

In his sorrow, Jacopone found his love shifting to the Divine when he discovered that before her death, his wife had had a secret love for God. He joined the Third Order of St. Francis and began to compose beautiful poems and hymns.

Stabat Mater, one of the most famous poems attributed to him, reflects on Mary and the suffering she must have experienced while watching her son Jesus die. The pain Jacopone felt is undoubtedly reflected in lyrics about Mary's sorrow: "Is there one who would not weep, whelm'd in miseries so deep."

Jacopone's lament is balanced by the healing praise he bestowed on his new love, Christ. "Love, You give light to the intellect in darkness and illumine the object of love," Jacopone writes. "Love, Your ardor, which enflames the heart, unites it with the Incarnate One."

Praise lifts the spirit. Whether we sing hymns written by others or create our own, finding the right words to express our love and gratitude toward God brings healing. It also sets us in the right attitude with God. "Let us continually offer to God a sacrifice of praise," says the writer of Hebrews (13:15).

Although worship is limited to God alone, praise is not. Bestowing praise on others is a form of encouragement. The more we use the muscles of praise and thanksgiving, the stronger they become. Praise is not the opposite of sorrow, as Jacopone's life and words show us. As we practice praise, it begins to permeate our every fiber.

Praise and glory to you, Beloved One, for bringing us out of darkness and filling our hearts with infinite intensity. I sing with Jacopone and the Psalmist: "Weeping may stay for the night, but rejoicing comes in the morning" (Ps 30:5). Amen.

LIGHT OF INFINITE INTENSITY GLOWS IN MY HEART
IESUS CHRISTUS
JACOPONE DA TODI

JEANNE GUYON (1648–1717) Praying Scripture

All Scripture is God-breathed. —2 Timothy 3:16

Madame Jeanne Guyon was a French Christian who spent almost twenty-five years imprisoned for her religious beliefs. During this time, she wrote devotional literature, including a book entitled *Experiencing the Depths of Jesus Christ*. In it, she offers the reader a form of contemplative engagement and a method for inner worship: "praying the scripture" and "beholding the Lord." Guyon writes, "In 'praying the scripture,' you are seeking to find the Lord in what you are reading, in the very words themselves."

We can engage with Scripture in prayerful, transformational, and educational ways. Guyon suggests a slow, meditative form of reading, sometimes limiting yourself to just a verse or two. Rather than skimming the surface, Guyon wrote, we can be like a "bee who penetrates into the depths of the flower." The exercise is for receiving revelation: divine communion with God. "The Scriptures point to me," Jesus states (John 5:39 NLT). And it's precisely this experience that Guyon encourages.

She also suggests using Scripture to quiet the mind. Meditating on the word, which is "alive and active," ushers us into the presence of the Living Word. At the moment we are aware of God's presence, reading is no longer required, for it has accomplished its goal.

The discipline, however, is to keep the mind in this state of awareness. While our thoughts will wander, Guyon suggests that we can avoid entertaining or indulging them. And as we develop a deeper prayer life, our mystical experiences unfold with greater frequency.

Like many mystics, Guyon advocated for a constant inner prayer life. Praying with scripture offers us a constant connection with the Divine, an inward stillness that can sustain and strengthen us at all times.

Living Word, thank you for your Holy Scriptures, your logos, and for Your Spirit who inspires them. Enlighten my mind and transform my soul. I pray I experience a deeper connection with you as you reveal your heart. Amen.

now I seek that constant prayer, in inward stillness known
Jeanne Guyon

JEAN-PIERRE DE CAUSSADE (1675–1751) Presence

Therefore do not worry about tomorrow, for tomorrow will worry about itself. Each day has enough trouble of its own.

—Matthew 6:34

Little is known about the French Jesuit priest Jean-Pierre de Caussade, but he is often credited with writing the letters that would become the book *Abandonment to Divine Providence*, also titled *The Sacrament of the Present Moment.* Authorship of the book has come under scrutiny in recent years; nonetheless, the spiritual director—whoever it maybe—presents helpful advice for our spiritual journey.

Being attentive to the will of God in humble obedience is what Jean-Pierre espouses. "The present moment is always full of infinite treasure," he assures us. We listen and act. Through this process of being present, our faith grows. God presents opportunities for creative and loving service and interaction. By obeying the Spirit's promptings, we will find that our love for God increases.

Trusting God's providence, as opposed to our own efforts, refreshes and empowers the soul. "All that is required for the sanctification of our soul comes from God's unconditional love for us," writes author Susan Muto. "We need to abandon ourselves to it like marble to a sculptor's chisel." Total reliance upon God leads us to the sacramental quality of the present. Surrendering requires humility, and even getting to that point is an act of God's grace; it requires "the hand of God to support and carry us to complete self-abandonment," Jean-Pierre writes.

Jesus lived a life of submission to the Father—moment by moment. Despite being rushed to heal an important official's daughter, he was attentive to a woman who touched the hem of his garment. Conversely, he left a group needing healing to preach his kingdom message in another town. Jesus escaped people pleasing because there was only One he needed to please.

Walking hand in hand with God today, we may find, as Jean-Pierre did, that all our moments manifest God's love.

God of the present, help me escape worry about the things of tomorrow and regret about the past by tuning in to your frequency. Amen.

EVERYTHING IS HEAVEN TO ME, BECAUSE ALL MY MOMENTS MANIFEST YOUR LOVE
Jean Pierre De Caussade

CHARLES ALBERT TINDLEY (1851–1933) Protest

He replied, "You of little faith, why are you so afraid?" Then he got up and rebuked the winds and the waves, and it was completely calm.

—MATTHEW 8:26

"When the storms of life are raging, stand by me," Charles Albert Tindley writes in one of his hymns. Known as the "grandfather of gospel music," Tindley was certainly acquainted with raging storms. His parents were enslaved, and Tindley himself was born into slavery. By the age of seventeen, three years after the Emancipation Proclamation, Tindley had taught himself reading and writing and was taking night classes toward becoming a minister.

In 1902, Tindley took over the reins as lead pastor at the Bainbridge Street Methodist Episcopal Church—Tindley Temple United Methodist Church today—in Philadelphia. Under his guidance, the congregation grew to 12,500 people of various racial and ethnic identities. Tindley also wrote hymns inspired by the early spirituals, forty-eight in all. His songs—including "Take Your Burden to the Lord," "When the Storms of Life Are Raging," and "I'll Overcome Some Day" (rewritten as a protest song during the civil rights movement to "We Shall Overcome")—continue to be sung today.

Tindley and a fellow minister peacefully picketed the racist 1915 movie *Birth of a Nation*. The movie portrays the Ku Klux Klan as a heroic force, protecting white women and preserving American values. Both ministers were beaten by a white mob, with Tindley sustaining injuries and his friend, Rev. Wesley Graham, being hospitalized.

Tindley had only begun to chip away at a racist system. Yet even after his death, his songs encourage future generations. Protest and praise unite within his life and work. May they unite in ours as well.

Judge of the nations; I sing in harmony with all my siblings in Christ the praises of your glory. Strengthen me to protest injustice. Make mercy and justice the wings to carry us onward and upward to reconciliation. Amen.

CHARLES ALBERT TINDLEY
MY SOUL IS FILLED WITH PRAISES

All this is from God, who reconciled us to himself through Christ and gave us the ministry of reconciliation.

—2 Corinthians 5:18

Dr. John M. Perkins traveled a long road: from a Mississippi sharecropper's son with a third-grade education to a man of faith who counseled five presidents and garnered numerous honorary doctorate degrees.

The road was not an easy one. Perkins's mother died of malnutrition when he was just an infant, and his dad abandoned him. At seventeen, he witnessed the murder of his brother by a police officer. Twenty-four years later, officers brutally beat him after he tried to bail out students who had participated in a boycott. That beating caused severe physical issues that he carries with him to this day.

Most people would be bitter. But here's what Perkins says: "Almost immediately God began to do something radical in my heart. He began to challenge my prejudices and my hatred toward others. I had learned to hate the white people in Mississippi . . . and if I had not met Jesus I would have died carrying that heavy burden of hate to my grave. But he began to strip it away, layer by layer."

Perkins committed his life to the ministry of reconciliation. "This is a God-sized problem," he writes. Then quoting G. K. Chesterton, he says, "It isn't that they [people in the church] can't see the solution. It is that they can't see the problem." He concludes, "One of the most important things we can do to move the cause of reconciliation forward is to pray for the brothers and sisters who we have been separate from."

As a sharecropper's son, Dr. John M. Perkins planted seeds in the rich Mississippi mud. As a leader of immense moral vision, he planted seeds of reconciliation that are now beginning to bear fruit.

God of unity, reconcile us to those from whom we've been separated. Make us of one mind, heart, and body. Plant a mustard seed in us to nurture and grow as we become the kingdom of heaven here on earth. Help us always end up with love. Amen.

John Perkins
Love. No matter where I start, I always end up here.

If we confess our sins, he is faithful and just and will forgive us our sins and purify us from all unrighteousness.

—1 John 1:9

Mary of Egypt, who was perhaps the victim of early sexual abuse, became a prostitute at age twelve. Whatever occurred to her in her youth, Mary left home with a desire to find love and acceptance. If what the Scottish writer Bruce Marshall suggests is true—that "the young man who rings the bell at the brothel is unconsciously looking for God"—then the woman working at the brothel is seeking the same.

Mary traveled to Jerusalem, paying for her voyage with sexual favors. While there, she intended to seduce men on pilgrimage—an "antipilgrimage," of sorts. Eventually, she tried to enter the Church of the Holy Sepulcher but was unable, seemingly held back by an unseen force.

John the Baptist and Jesus both came preaching repentance: to turn away from a harmful life and move toward the fruitful life only God can give. Mary's life illustrates this well. When she attempted to enter the church again, this time she was successful. Passing through the doorway, Mary approached the true cross—the one said to be the exact cross on which Jesus hung. She knelt before it and laid the burden—the sins she committed and those committed against her—there.

Back outside, Mary heard a voice from an icon of the Madonna: "If you cross the Jordan, you will find glorious rest." Rest! Rest from being used, and rest from striving. She took these words quite literally and departed for the desert.

Mary's years spent in the wilderness would not be easy. But the many years of desperately longing for fulfillment, of trying to find love, were now over. Matthew 11:28 holds a great promise. "Come to me, all you who are weary and burdened," Jesus pleads, to Mary and to us, "and I will give you rest."

O Most Merciful One, forgive my sins: what I have done and what I have left undone. By your Son's sacrificial gift, I lay my burdens at the cross. Your love and acceptance bring me comfort and a place I can call home. Amen.

BLESSED IS GOD WHO CARES FOR THE SALVATION OF ALL SOULS
Mary of Egypt

We also glory in our sufferings, because we know that suffering produces perseverance; perseverance, character; and character, hope.

—Romans 5:3–4

By some historians' accounts, there were twice as many desert mothers as fathers in the Egyptian wasteland during the early part of Christendom. Yet Amma Theodora is only one of a handful of desert mothers whose sayings have survived. In the desert, women could lead and share their wisdom in ways that they often couldn't when they were living in areas in which church leadership could thwart their gifts.

In the often dense ancient Apophthegmata writings—when it seems the desert sages went too long without food or water in the scorching heat—Theodora's down-to-earth wisdom shines through.

Amma Theodora tells us, "Just as the trees, if they have not stood before the winter's storms cannot bear fruit, so it is with us." Trees fall to the wayside if they haven't developed a deeply rooted system. Muscles without exercise begin to atrophy. Physical therapists will tell you that resistance is needed to regain strength and develop a healthy working body. Amma Theodora reminds us that it's no different for the spiritual life: diversity is required to create optimal function. Hardship breeds resilience.

Amma Syncletica, a contemporary of Amma Theodora, states, "Those who are great athletes must contend with stronger enemies." During our lives, we will encounter our demons. And trials and tribulations will come. But we can relinquish these battles to an even stronger Advocate.

"Resilient people, those who have come through difficulty well, report a journey that has a moral direction," writes Justine Allain-Chapman in *The Resilient Disciple*. "It starts in adversity and ends in altruism, for the fruits of the journey of suffering are experienced as compassion for others and healing for oneself."

The desert mothers show us the way of resilience—of moving from adversity to altruism.

Grant to me, my Beloved, a resilient heart. Lift me in times of weariness. Empower me in weakness, and deliver me from death's defeat. Amen.

WINTER STORMS PRODUCE FRUIT-BEARING TREES; SO IT IS WITH US
AMMA THEODORA

AMBROSE OF MILAN (374–397) Rest

In repentance and rest is your salvation, in quietness and trust is your strength.

—Isaiah 30:15

God worked for six days and rested on the seventh. One of the Ten Commandments tells us to rest from our labors on the Sabbath. Since Jesus has become our Sabbath rest, the Sabbath is no longer a required law, but it is still a gift. "We especially care for the seed of eternity planted in the soul," Abraham Joshua Heschel reminds us.

As we carry the heavy burden of workdays filled with responsibilities, chores, and deadlines, St. Ambrose, the bishop of Milan, offers us some key concepts. He states, "To rest in the Lord and to see his joy is like a banquet, full of gladness and tranquility."

But finding times and places of rest can be difficult, especially for people with family and job commitments. Assessing our season of life—and knowing that seasons change—can be instrumental in moving deeper into rest. Sabbath rest doesn't always look like intercessory prayer or reading through the Bible or silent retreats. Sometimes it looks like meditating on a line of Scripture or praying in the car on your way to work. In small moments of the day, we can create a Sabbath refuge.

Ambrose offers great insight into this sanctuary of shalom. "Your soul must hold fast to him, you must follow after him in your thoughts . . . you must take refuge in him," he states. We can learn to simply rest in God, doing nothing more than what Mother Teresa advises: "I look at [Christ] and he looks at me."

Resting in God becomes an entire banquet of sweetness, joy, and tranquility.

Lord of the Sabbath, bring rest to weary travelers, release to burdened servants, and order to harried lives. Peace you leave with us; peace you give to us. Amen.

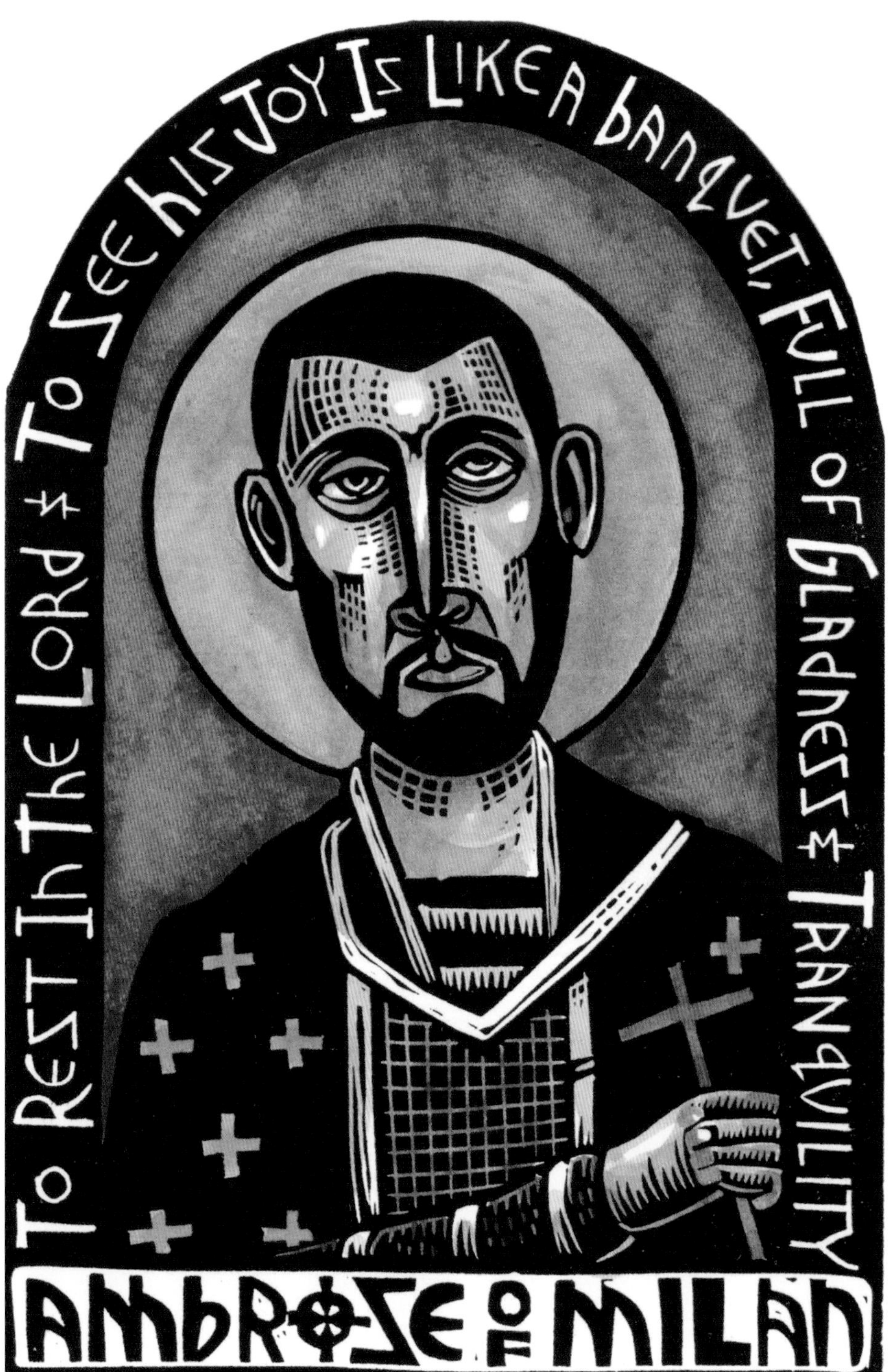
To rest in the Lord + To see his joy is like a banquet, full of gladness + tranquility
Ambrose of Milan

But Christ has indeed been raised from the dead, the firstfruits of those who have fallen asleep.

—1 CORINTHIANS 15:20

Death is the great unknown. The great equalizer. During the medieval ages, death was portrayed in the arts as a skeleton, leveling kings while bringing relief to the impoverished. One day our own hearts will cease beating and our bodies will return to dust. Ashes to ashes, dust to dust.

But the mystery of Christ is the resurrected life, now and after death. St. John Chrysostom, the archbishop of Constantinople, reminds us of this hope: "O Death, where is your sting? O Hell, where is your victory? Christ is risen, and you are overthrown." Within the Orthodox Church, on Easter Sunday, the Paschal Homily of Chrysostom is read at matins, which occurs in the early morning. Then Chrysostom's Divine Liturgy is celebrated. "Let no one weep for his iniquities, for pardon has shown forth from the grave," he encourages us. "Let no one fear death, for the Savior's death has set us free."

Have we tasted a love that brings a longing to our souls? How many of us can say with St. Paul in Philippians 1:23, "I desire to depart and be with Christ, which is better by far"? How many of us have had a resurrection experience that drives us onward?

With faith, through darkened days and moments of sunshine, through times of doubt and blessed assurance, we hold fast to the divine sown within—Christ in us, the hope of glory! We embrace what Chrysostom so eloquently preached: "Christ is risen, and the angels rejoice. Christ is risen, and life reigns. Christ is risen, and not one dead remains in the grave. For Christ, being risen from the dead is become the first fruits of those who have fallen asleep. To Him be glory and dominion unto ages of ages."

Christ, our resurrection and life, restore to me that which is dead. Bring life to these limbs, light to this soul, and joy in your eternal plan. Amen.

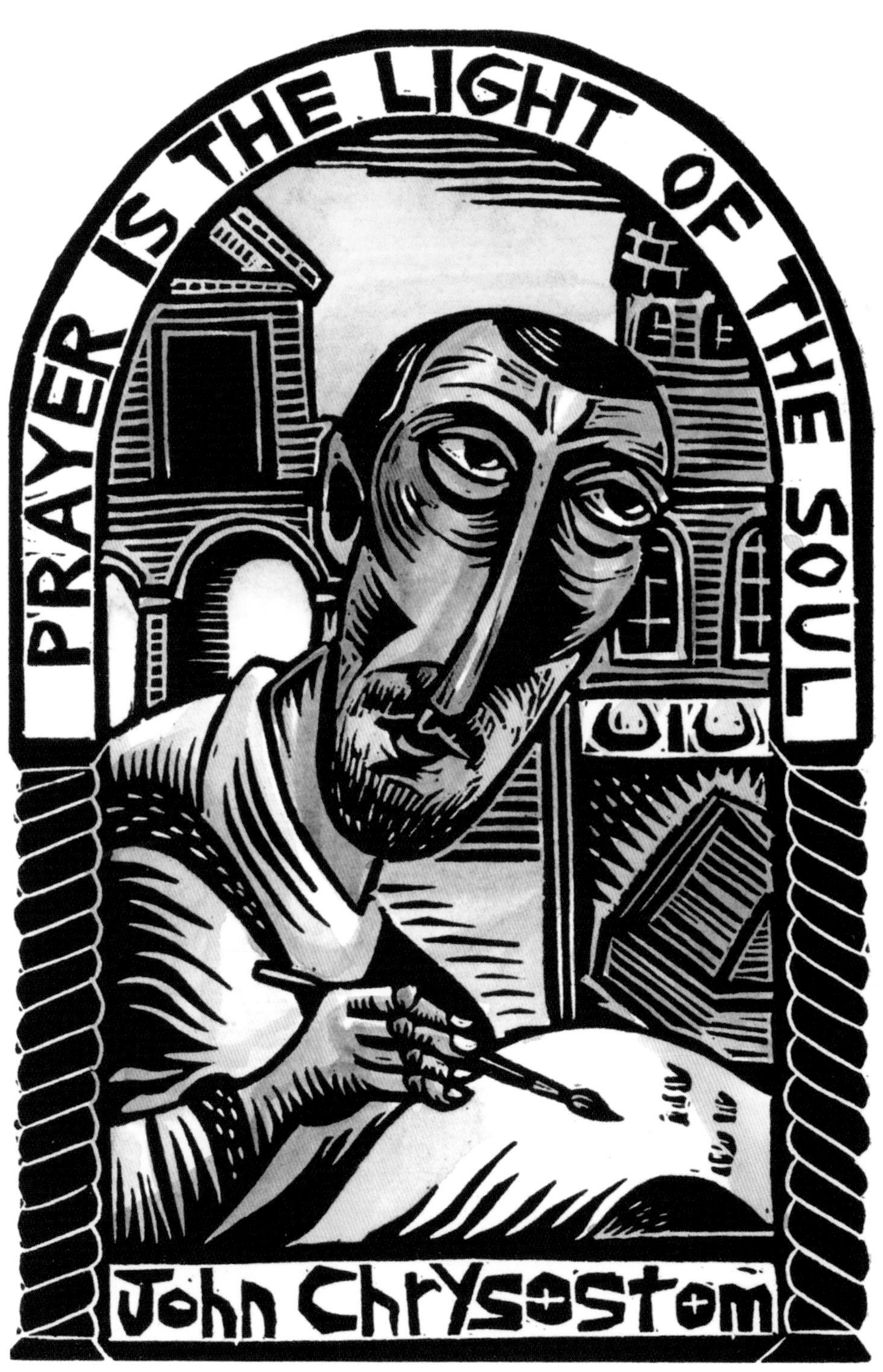
PRAYER IS THE LIGHT OF THE SOUL
John Chrysostom

There is a time for everything, and a season for every activity under the heavens.
—ECCLESIASTES 3:1

Brother Victor-Antoine D'Avila-Latourrette lived in a village in the Pyrénées mountains in France before moving to upstate New York and becoming a monk. As a Benedictine, he lived a life of routine: the Canonical Hours of daily prayer, liturgy, recreation, eating, work, and rest. His duties were to tend the gardens and care for the animals at Our Lady of the Resurrection Monastery.

One need not be a monk to benefit from a monk's life-sustaining habits. Our bodies have been created to observe natural rhythms. Sabbath rest days are essential. We retreat during winter and expend more energy with the long summer days. We require solitude as much as we need community. Attending to a balanced diet and movement and routine, based on our own unique design, results in physical and spiritual health.

One of the principles at the monastery, Brother Victor-Antoine said, was "to synchronize [the] planting schedule with the rhythms of the liturgy." He lived off the land, cooking fresh produce grown in the small monastery garden: beans, potatoes, cabbage, lettuce, tomatoes, zucchini, Swiss chard, and more. Numerous cookbooks of his soup recipes soon followed, as did meditative books on the monastic life.

In his devotional, *Walk in His Ways*, Brother Victor-Antoine describes in detail the changing seasons: the lengthening shadows, the first approaching coolness of autumn, the luminous skies. Just as the changing seasons presented Brother Victor-Antoine with a routine for physical work, the liturgical cycle and the Christian calendar offered him a spiritual pattern. He writes, "Monastic life is organized around a life-giving rhythm: the daily celebration of the work of God . . . prayer, adoration, the praise of God."

Finding our own unique rhythm begins with this essential element: daily prayer. Brother Victor-Antoine reminds us that whether we're a monastic or layperson, our rhythm of life "grows in silence and solitude and is nourished daily by reading, meditation, and much prayer."

Spirit of the seasons, synchronize my heart with yours. Through a balanced work schedule and rest pattern—one that nourishes body, soul, and spirit—conform me into your image. Amen.

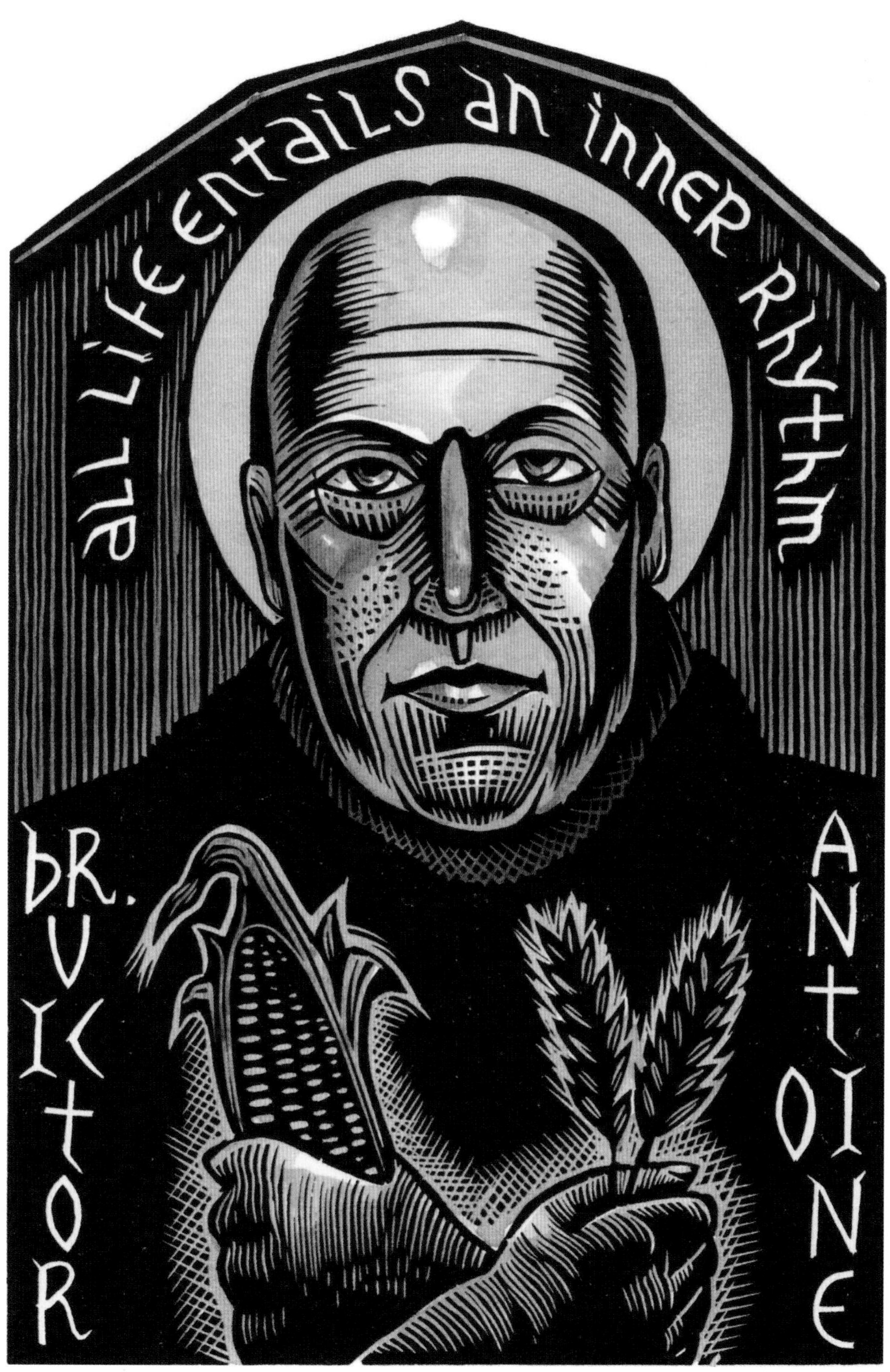
all life entails an inner rhythm
br. victor
antoine

Lord, teach us to pray. —LUKE 11:1

The German theologian Martin Luther will always be known as the man who nailed his *Ninety-Five Theses* to the door of a church in Wittenberg. That legend may be true—or not. In any case, we know that Luther took on the corruption of the church in his day, sending a great, quaking shudder through the body of Christ that became known as the Protestant Reformation.

Luther was a reformer and a monk, but above all else, he was a man of prayer. Singing the Psalter was his daily bread. In a 1535 booklet titled *A Simple Way to Pray*, he advised readers to use various Scriptures and creeds in their prayer lives: the Psalms, portions of the New Testament, the Ten Commandments, the Apostles' Creed, and the Our Father. He suggests we approach the readings as "a garland of four strands": instruction, thanksgiving, confession, and prayer.

Prayer can be the first thing we do in the morning and the last before nodding off to sleep. "I suckle at the Lord's Prayer like a child," Luther confides, "and as an old man, eat and drink from it and never get my fill."

While Luther's "rule of prayer" will not be for everyone, creating a consistent prayer life is essential. We learn to pray by praying. "None can believe how powerful prayer is, and what it is able to effect," says Luther, "except those who have learned it by experience."

What's important is to find a way of praying that suits you. Some people prefer praying prayers from Scripture or the historic and global church, while others simply say to God whatever comes to mind. Some prefer to pray alone and others in groups. Physical posture can enhance prayer: walking, standing with arms raised, sitting, kneeling, or lying down.

What suits you in one season might change in the next. Be flexible, experiment, and be gentle with yourself. But most importantly: keep praying. Like one of the disciples did, we can even ask Jesus to teach us how to pray.

O Ruler of my life, you've made each of us unique, and you connect with us in your own special way. Lord, teach me to pray. Amen.

MAKE THEE A BED UNDEFILED WITHIN MY HEART, A QUIET CHAMBER KEPT FOR THEE
Martin Luther

For them I sanctify myself, that they too may be truly sanctified.

—JOHN 17:19

Sanctification—*hagiasmos*, in Greek—means consecration or purification. It's the act of making or declaring something holy. The idea of becoming sanctified—being made holy—has permeated Christian thinking since ancient times.

Today we might be more apt to speak in terms of the "false self" (the unsanctified version) and the "true self" (the sanctified one). Whatever we call it, the sanctified self is what God created us to be: pure, peaceable, authentic, and loving.

Symeon the New Theologian was an Eastern Orthodox monk and poet who often described his experience of God as divine light. In his writing, he admonishes us to strive for such things but to remember God's grace. "It is not possible for us to become holy and to be saints in an hour!" he declares—to which we breathe a sigh of relief. Fully living in Christlikeness takes a lifetime—and then some!

St. Paul encourages us to train in such a way as if we were running a long distance. "Run in such a way as to get the prize," he encourages us (1 Cor 9:24). But here's the kicker: we never reach the finish line! "Even were we to spend a thousand years in this life, we should never perfectly attain [holiness]," Symeon assures us. "Rather, we must always struggle for it every day as if mere beginners."

Sanctification sometimes gets a bad rap. Because of many failed examples—people who claimed to be sanctified and clearly aren't—some have come to see it as snobbery. But this couldn't be further from the truth. Like Christ, the true self does not look down on others or judge them. The true self offers healing and looks for the best in others.

We are called to be a "holy people," St. Peter reminds us (1 Pet 1:16). And who better to continue this work than the Holy Spirit? Holiness, through sanctification, is the finish line. We are both *already* holy and *still being made* holy. Sanctification is a work of God's grace.

O Sun that never sets, sanctify me for your purposes: a pure and holy vessel that carries within it the Divine Spirit. Amen.

you are a light that knows no evening a sun that never sets
SYMEON THE THEOLOGIAN

But the fruit of the Spirit is . . . self-control. —GALATIANS 5:22–23

We are all prone to addiction. Whether it's alcohol, nicotine, caffeine, food, possessions, television, pornography, social media, gaming, or something else: unchecked desires can dominate our lives.

Saint Dominic, the founder of the Dominican monastic order who lived in what is present-day Spain, states, "A man who governs his passions is master of his world. We must either command them or be enslaved by them." The discipline of self-control, one of the nine fruits of the Spirit that Saint Paul introduced in his letter to the Galatians, combats addictive behavior at the root.

Self-control is about moderation. It's also about love for oneself—not hating one's body in a way that brings about fanatical asceticism or harm.

Jesus spoke of hatred and lust emanating from one's heart long before the actual act of murder or adultery occurs. An initial seed of temptation may or may not take root, depending on our response. Do we take every thought captive before it has a chance to grow? Or do we allow temptation to flourish? Redirecting our attention toward what is pure, praiseworthy, and nondestructive is the first step toward victory.

Another monk, Thomas à Kempis, advises, "Do not let the enemy enter the door of your heart." Slick advertisers know this strategy all too well! Thomas continues, "Temptation works in this way: First, an unrighteous thought creeps into your mind. Next, your imagination takes hold of the idea. Then you begin to delight in the thought of the action. Finally, you consent."

Dominic advises us to wield "prayer rather than a sword." We offer up our struggles to God, and we pray for the Spirit's empowerment. And we take positive and active means to find solutions. "It is better to be a hammer than an anvil," he continues. In other words, govern your addiction before it governs you.

Spirit of self-control, give me the discipline I need to make positive changes in my life. Empower me in ways to overcome what is harmful to me and others. By your mercy, I pray. Amen.

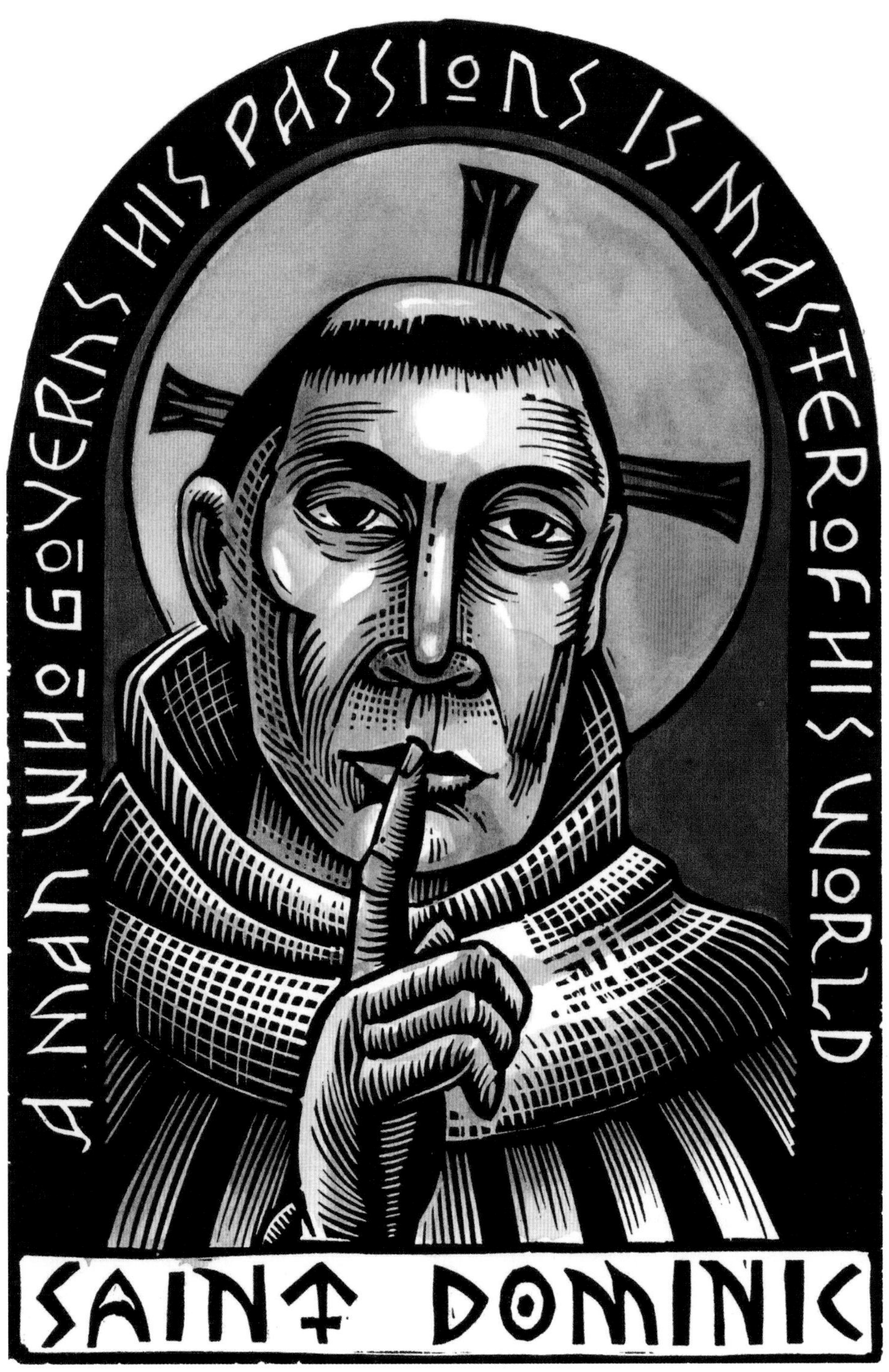
A MAN WHO GOVERNS HIS PASSIONS IS MASTER OF HIS WORLD
SAINT DOMINIC

The greatest among you will be your servant. —MATTHEW 23:11

Saint Teresa of Calcutta, better known as Mother Teresa, founded the Missionaries of Charity, which serves the impoverished in Calcutta. She felt called by God to care for people who were outcasts and unwanted—those that many in society deemed unacceptable. Teresa initially started with nothing—doing what she could, asking for help, and delivering care where desperately needed. Teresa became, for the people, a connection to God.

"Do not look for spectacular works," Teresa admits. "What is important is the gift of ourselves." Her small gift would have ripple effects as the ministry grew worldwide. The Missionaries of Charity built shelters for people experiencing homelessness and those with drug addiction. They brought relief to areas reeling from natural disasters—flood, famine, hurricane—and refugee relocation. In 1969, Coworkers formed, providing a means for laypersons to assist the religious order, adding yet another element to what she had begun.

The evening before Jesus died, he wished to impart an essential teaching to his disciples. So Jesus got on his knees and began to wash their dirty feet. "You also should wash one another's feet," he instructs them. "I have set you an example" (John 13:14–15).

Mother Teresa washed the feet of the children in Calcutta. Like Jesus, she sets the bar extremely high. Yet great things are not what is required. And as Mother Teresa's letters showed us when they were published after her death, a feeling of God's presence is not always required either. She often felt far from God and had a hard time praying—but she didn't stop serving God. She reminds us, "What matters is not how much we do, but how much love we put in what we do."

Each of us has gifts to serve others. What we do with those gifts is up to us. How God multiplies and brings ripple effects is up to God.

Suffering Servant, I'm grateful for the gifts that you have given me: gifts that can be used to serve others, gifts that can create ripples in the sea of love. Make me a servant of others, and multiply each small effort I make. Amen.

BE THE LIVING EXPRESSION OF GOD'S KINDNESS
mother teresa

In quietness and trust is your strength. —Isaiah 30:15

Many of us find it difficult to find a place of silence. We live in a world of rampant noise: fast food chains blare music through loudspeakers, airplanes scorch the skies, and traffic noise begins our day. And yet somehow we're supposed to hear God, who is trying to speak to us in a gentle whisper?

"There is a huge silence inside each of us that beckons us into itself," says the German mystic Meister Eckhart, whose writings on the mysteries of faith continue to draw readers. "And the recovery of our own silence can begin to teach us the language of heaven." Recovering our silence can be difficult. But creating a space where this can occur is of utmost importance for our communion with the Divine.

"To let go of all agendas and settle into a deep silence is perhaps the most countercultural thing we can do," writes contemplative Amos Smith. "It requires trust that silence and stillness are indeed God's first language, and when we meet God on God's terms amazing things happen."

Meister Eckhart would agree. In the vast, primordial darkness of space, where the mystery of the Cosmic Christ dwells, we find our birth. "There is nothing so much like God in all the universe as silence," Eckhart says.

Jesus advises, "Find a quiet, secluded place. . . . You will begin to sense his grace" (Matt 6:6 MSG). Creating a "prayer closet"—some space away from the noise—can help. It might be a literal closet, the corner of a room, a den, or even the back stoop. Or a metaphorical one, in which you close your eyes. But setting aside a location for prayer alone makes this space sacred. A simple environment is advantageous: perhaps a lit candle, icon, prayer book, Bible—and maybe even earplugs.

There are many ways to retreat for prayer and cultivate the silence within. God will meet us there.

Heart of Silence, I know you communicate with me even when I don't always hear you. Help me to unplug from the constant barrage of noise and "recover my own silence," as Eckhart suggests. Help me to hear your gentle whisper and rest in your embracing love. Amen.

IT IS IN DARKNESS ONE FINDS THE LIGHT, IN SORROW. THIS LIGHT IS NEAREST TO US
MEISTER ECKHART

Blessed are you who are poor, for yours is the kingdom of God.

—Luke 6:20

Born of nobility, Chiara Offreduccio lived a life destined for marriage and wealth. But her life took an extreme turn when she witnessed the changed man Francis, who we know as St. Francis of Assisi, and heard his simple preaching.

Eventually, Chiara—known today as St. Clare of Assisi—settled at the monastery of San Damiano, which Francis had repaired with his hands, and formed a small community of like-minded women known as the Order of Poor Women. They took their vows to Christ and to a life of poverty and prayer. "Take care to distribute [your] proceeds to the poor," Clare writes in her Rule, always conscientious of those in need.

There's nothing romantic about poverty, Wendy Murray reminds us in her book, *Clare of Assisi: Gentle Warrior.* But she points out that poverty does often foster self-reflection, grace, humility, and a willingness to be despised. It often strengthens human will and removes the tendency to judge others.

Even if we don't embrace poverty to the extent that Clare did, we may still find benefits in relinquishing some of our possessions. With God as our Provider, our focus shifts from living the self-made life to one entirely dependent on God's grace.

St. Clare teaches us about giving more and taking less. She helps us learn to let go of material items, which allows for a simple, uncluttered way of living. To bless others becomes the spark that ignites others to do the same.

Bestower of Life, strip away from me that which I can do without, all that hinders our union. Help me live a calm and uncluttered life; as some have said, "To live simply, so others can simply live." Amen.

now go calmly in peace, for you have a good escort
Clare of Assisi

Love your neighbor as yourself. —LUKE 10:27

We must often choose between safety and solidarity. If someone is being treated cruelly and unfairly, we can choose our own safety, or we can choose to stand with them.

That was the choice Corrie ten Boom and her family faced. The Nazi regime had taken over Holland. Boys were being taken from the streets and forced to work. Jewish people were being rounded up and shipped off by train to undisclosed locations. The rumors began floating around: unimaginable stories, about death camps and torture.

Corrie, her sister, and their elderly father knew they had to make a decision: a dangerous decision that might cost them their own lives. They chose solidarity. "It is not my ability, but my response to God's ability that counts," Corrie acknowledges. They constructed a hiding place that harbored Jews while they worked to arrange for their escape.

When the Nazis discovered what the ten Booms were doing, they imprisoned Corrie's father, who died shortly thereafter. Corrie and her sister got shipped off to Ravensbrück concentration camp. There Corrie witnessed the death of her sister and other horrors. Yet she was able to proclaim what her sister had told her: "There is no pit so deep that God's love is not deeper still."

Jesus tells the story of a man who is beaten, stripped, robbed, and left for dead on the side of the road. Two religious men—a priest and a Levite—pass him by. Was this a setup? they must have wondered. Will they do the same to me if I stop to help? They had a decision to make, and they chose their own safety. A third man, a Samaritan outcast, came by and cared for the victim, bandaged his wounds, and found him a place to stay—all at personal cost.

The story's hero was not the priest or Levite but the one who loved his neighbor in tangible ways. Jesus says, "Go and do likewise."

God, my hiding place, give me empathy and courage to love even in difficult situations. Grant me wisdom and discernment in pursuing solidarity and pursuing your will. Amen.

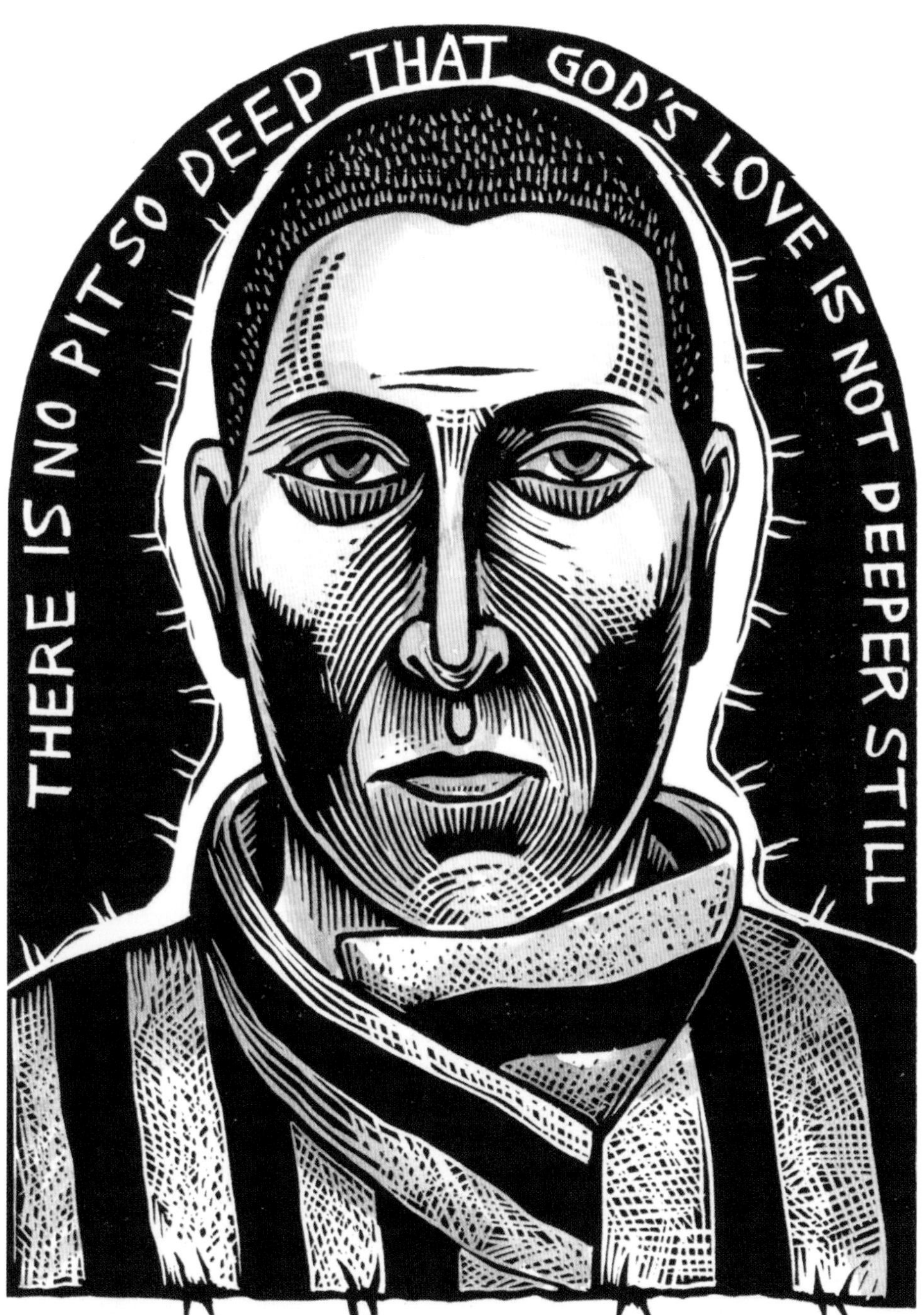

CORRIE TEN BOOM

SERAPHIM OF SAROV (1759–1833) Solitude

Come with me by yourselves to a quiet place and get some rest.

—Mark 6:31

Seraphim was a mystic, a monastic priest who lived as a hermit in the forest outside of Sarov, Russia. Immersed in the solitude and beauty of the solitary life for twenty-five years, he found peace with himself and with the world. During these moments of contemplation, he received many mystical encounters.

Like saints such as Kevin of Glendalough and Francis of Assisi, Seraphim lived in harmony with nature and the animal kingdom. One story tells of a visiting nun who found him sitting on a tree stump, feeding a bear. Seraphim sent the bear off and invited her to join him. Shortly, however, the bear returned. Seraphim, relaxed and peaceful, assured her all was well. She marveled as he helped her to feed the bear.

Years later, the nun passed by an iconographer's studio and saw him painting seraphim. "Don't forget the bear!" she exclaimed. Seraphim has been depicted that way ever since.

Jesus often retreated to the hills surrounding Galilee and encouraged his disciples to do the same. During these extended times of isolation, he communed with his Father and received insight for the following day.

If Jesus needed such times, we certainly need the same! Retreat and solitude are essential for renewal in our hectic world. A park bench, a walk in the woods, or a weekend monastic retreat can rejuvenate the soul—and tame the wild bear.

Many sought out seraphim for his wisdom and healing prayers. "Establish yourself in God," the monk encouraged them; "then you will be helpful to others." We can only give what we receive and only receive when we enter into prayer. Finding times of solitude, we are strengthened for the work at hand. "Acquire a peaceful spirit," says the hermit, "and thousands around you will be saved."

Prince of Peace, in the busyness of life—always doing, always working, always striving—remind me to just be. Lead me beside still waters; restore my soul. The peace you give me, may I give to others. Amen.

ESTABLISH YOURSELF IN GOD & THEN YOU WILL BE HELPFUL TO OTHERS
SERAPHIM OF SAROV

A friend loves at all times. —Proverbs 17:17

David and Jonathan, Ruth and Naomi, Jesus and his inner circle: these biblical friendships serve as examples of what close friends can become. The ancient Celtic Christians called this type of friend *anamchara*: soul friend. Having a spiritual connection with another on our journey through life is a gift. In this tight bond, we can find acceptance, encouragement, and an outlet for confession.

Finding a connection that can help us pursue our walk with Christ is what Cistercian monk Aelred of Rievaulx writes about in his book *On Spiritual Friendship*. This type of friendship has a deep dimension to it. "The reward of friendship is itself. The man who hopes for anything else does not understand what true friendship is," he says. Aelred notes that "worldly" friendship might be nothing more than a connection for financial gain. Likewise, a "carnal" friendship is merely superficial—good times and parties but rarely much depth. Such friendship is self-seeking: to find pleasure for oneself with veritable disregard for the other.

True soul friendship, however, is derived through mutual respect, pursuit, honesty, and commitment. It has an added element—the spiritual dimension—that brings God into the equation. "My friend must be the guardian of our mutual love, or even of my very soul," writes Aelred, "so that he will preserve in faithful silence all its secrets, and whatever he sees in it that is flawed he will correct or endure with all his strength."

Ultimately, Jesus is our soul friend, and he models spiritual friendship. Jesus tells his disciples, "I no longer call you servants. . . . I have called you friends" (John 15:15).

Finding a soul friend can't be forced. Many variables come into play. But finding someone who can share the intimacy of your faith, dreams, values, and interests is a true gift.

O Beloved Bridegroom, you are the bond of my spiritual friendships, you are our pursuit. Bring friends into my life to challenge, encourage, and transform me into Christlikeness, and help me to reciprocate this love. Amen.

When i wander from you, within me i find darkness and fear.
Aelred of Rievaulx

Guide me in your truth and teach me. —PSALM 25:5

In the English village of Norwich sits a modest stone church with a small cell attached. In this room lived the Benedictine mystic and spiritual director we refer to as Julian of Norwich. During plague and famine, her message of God's love perplexed many. Yet her suffering lent authority to her words.

Sixteen mystical visions, which followed a near-death experience at age thirty, brought her greater clarity and insight. She immediately wrote down the visions, along with commentary, and wrote a second book after meditating on their meaning. These visions in her book *Showings*, or *Revelations of Divine Love*, are the earliest surviving works by a female English writer.

In one of the visions, she saw a "little thing" the size of a hazelnut in her hand. She wondered what this could be and received an answer: "It is all that is made." The object seemed so fragile and small that Julian wondered if it could easily be lost. "It lasts and ever shall, for God loves it," was the reply.

At a time when medieval spirituality focused on God's wrath and human sinfulness, Julian's counsel must have come as a breath of fresh air to her directees. Julian wanted to suffer as a means of intimacy with Jesus, the suffering servant; yet through these trials, God spoke to her of healing, comfort, and direction—not of pain and condemnation. She writes, "Mercy is a sweet work of love, mingled with abundant pity, for mercy works to keep us and turn all things into good."

Julian was one of the first writers to refer to God as a Mother. "You are our clothing; for love, you wrap us and embrace us," she writes. And also: "We are so preciously loved by [you] that we cannot even comprehend it."

While the world fell apart around her, Julian saw people in desperate need and pain. She still managed to say: "All shall be well, and all shall be well, and all manner of things shall be well."

Beloved Christ, at times I'm still afraid and doubt. Strengthen my faith and help me to trust that all manner of things shall be well. Amen.

ALL SHALL BE WELL & ALL SHALL BE WELL & ALL MANNER OF THINGS SHALL BE WELL
JULIAN OF NORWICH

My dear children, for whom I am again in the pains of childbirth until Christ is formed in you.

—Galatians 4:19

The French spiritual director Francis de Sales encourages a disciplined devotional life that constantly moves "toward the love of God." Whether in good times or bad, we face a choice: will we move toward the love of God or away from it?

In Francis's book *Introduction to the Devout Life*, he presents a balanced plan of attack for spiritual formation. Prayer and the Eucharist form the foundation that the disciple can build upon. Francis addresses spiritual dryness, anger, self-reproach, and other setbacks, giving possible solutions for each. Through the spiritual formation process, we aim to constantly deepen and become more our true selves: loving and Christlike.

This long, arduous journey is circular, not linear. Spiritual formation is less like a race route and more like a labyrinth, where sometimes we're closer to the center, occasionally further away, but always moving toward that center.

The gentle spiritual director is aware of this. "Don't dwell upon your lack of perfection," Francis encourages us; "there is no value in harsh, dismal, rancorous, and emotional disapproval of yourself." Instead, we seek God's mercy, lean on God's direction, and begin again. Spiritual growth involves moving toward divine mercy each day.

Patience and humility are two virtues Francis finds essential. Our progress flounders without them. These virtues often blossom in times of adversity. Francis addresses the reader who might find his proposal difficult and painful: "Once you begin to live the devout life," he says, "you will find it to be extraordinarily pleasant."

We can make ourselves wholly available daily. Francis suggests "examining and servicing our hearts" annually, taking a "spiritual inventory," and renewing our vows on important dates. Spiritual formation occurs by the grace of God working in and through us.

Great Potter, mold me into my true self, the person you've created me to be. Help me to believe all things work together for good according to your purposes. Amen.

God, whose very own you are, will lead you safely through all things
FRANCIS de SALES

JOHN OF THE CROSS (1542–1591) Spiritual Maturity

Now for a little while you may have had to suffer grief in all kinds of trials. These have come so that the proven genuineness of your faith . . . may result in praise, glory and honor when Jesus Christ is revealed.

—1 Peter 1:7

When you feel far from God, some Christians might suggest that it's your problem. The believer is the one who must be at fault, because God is always with us, right?

The poet, priest, and Carmelite monk Juan de Yepes y Álvarez suggests that something deeper is going on during times when you can't feel God's presence.

Juan—who would come to be known as St. John of the Cross—was trying to reform the Carmelite order. Monks who disagreed with him took him as a prisoner and held him captive at a monastery in Spain. During this time John felt abandoned by God. He experienced the depth of the suffering of Christ in an intimate way—what he referred to as "the dark night of the soul."

Today people often use this phrase to refer to a crisis of faith. But that wasn't John's intention. The "dark night" is when God removes all crutches and favors. We become unable to rely on our feelings or even sense God's presence. What is left is only a void. The dark night of the soul is the final purging and maturing of the self.

John readies his reader by stating, "As fire consumes the tarnish and rust of metal, this contemplation annihilates, empties and consumes all the affections and imperfect habits the soul contracted throughout its life."

We love God and God alone—not the feelings of joy or inner peace. We walk by faith and not by feeling. If you undergo your own dark night of the soul, know that others have endured it too. In this final stage of spiritual maturity, John assures us, "The endurance of darkness is the preparation for great light."

Faithful One, you know the feeling of abandonment. You carry the suffering of us all. Be a light in my darkness, and strengthen my faith when feelings won't come and all seems hopeless and lost. Amen.

GENTLY & LOVINGLY YOU WAKE IN MY HEART, WHERE IN SECRET YOU DWELL ALONE
John of the Cross

For our struggle is not against flesh and blood, but against the rulers, against the authorities, against the powers of this dark world and the spiritual forces of evil in the heavenly realms.

—EPHESIANS 6:12

Abba Antony became the ascetic ideal for many men and women sojourning into the desert wasteland. He heard and heeded the call to live a gospel life, separating himself from all that kept him from God and journeying toward God. His location in the Egyptian desert offered him the isolation needed for his formidable opponent: the devil. Antony warns us, "Expect temptation to [your] last breath."

Desolate and barren landscapes often mirror our spiritual geography, creating a thirst for the rivers of God's grace. Silence can strip away our need for people's approval.

Spiritual warfare was very real to Antony, as it had been with Jesus in the wilderness. "Put on the full armor of Christ," St. Paul admonishes, "so that you can take your stand against the devil's schemes."

Fifteenth-century printmaker Martin Schongauer depicted Abba Antony's spiritual battles. In the print, Antony is caught up in the air, wrestling with his demons—colorful reptilian conglomerations of body, fin, and wing.

The concept of spiritual warfare might be disconcerting to some contemporary readers. "Spiritual forces of evil in the heavenly realms" might sound strange to our ears. Yet as we journey through our spiritual landscape, we are bound to confront powers that confound and destroy.

Antony leaves us with this bit of wisdom: "Whoever you may be, always have God before your eyes; Whatever you do, do it according to the testimony of the holy Scriptures; In whatever place you live, do not easily leave it. Keep these three precepts and you will be saved."

Christ in the wilderness, as I sojourn into places unknown—the road less traveled—be my guide. When I'm uncertain, when affliction comes, I take comfort in knowing you are there and you are my strength to fight against evil. Amen.

always have God before your eyes wherever you go
ABBA ANTONY

ATHANASIUS OF ALEXANDRIA (293–373) Steadfastness

Therefore, my dear brothers and sisters, stand firm. Let nothing move you.

—1 Corinthians 15:58

Saint Athanasius was steadfast in his conviction. He agreed with John's claim that Jesus Christ "was with God in the beginning. Through him all things were made; without him nothing was made that has been made" (John 1:2–3). And he did not deviate from this path. He opposed Arianism, a theology that maintained that Christ was not coeternal. These debates, and others, would get him exiled five times from Alexandria. He'd be even more committed to his creed each time he returned.

Athanasius, who was a bishop, often retreated to the desert regions during these exiles. While breaking bread with the desert monks, he found that the extended time in solitude strengthened his resolve and refreshed his spirit. He wrote his bestseller on Abba Antony, a man who fought and triumphed over his own demons, on one of his visits to the desert.

Returning to Alexandria in 325, Athanasius played a significant role in writing the Nicene Creed—a confession of the faith that still shapes Christian theology: "God from God, Light from Light, true God from true God, begotten, not made, consubstantial with the Father; through him all things were made." Athanasius is said to have also confirmed the twenty-seven books of the New Testament as Scripture, although they wouldn't be formally canonized until twenty years after his death.

The steadfastness of Athanasius laid the next stone on the cornerstone. "We were the purpose of his embodiment," he declares, "and for our salvation he so loved human beings as to come to be and appear in a human body"—a mystery of unsurpassable worth.

Our steadfast resolutions must be grounded in humility and truth. As we see in Jesus's encounters with the Pharisees, dogmatism isn't always commendable! We can build on a foundation while still being willing to adjust our errors. We can hold fast to God's certainties, not our own.

Rock of Ages, you are the Mystery incarnate: Emmanuel, God with us. Help me to build on this rock, to relinquish falsehood, and to be steadfast to the truth while facing opposition. Amen.

JESUS BECAME WHAT WE ARE THAT HE MIGHT
MAKE US WHAT HE IS
ATHANASIUS

Be still and know that I am God. —Psalm 46:10

The world often seems out of control. Often we go from noise to noise, activity to activity. Social media and digital communication make demands on our attention and time. Throw in a few global crises—wars, gun violence, climate change, rising economic worries—and you have a ready-made mental health crisis. A report by the American Psychological Association suggests that those between the ages of fifteen and twenty-one generally experience a higher level of stress and anxiety than previous generations did.

Can an eighteenth-century German mystic offer any helpful advice? "Do not think anymore and allow yourself to go into God's inmost place," writes Gerhard Tersteegen, a writer, poet, and pastor. "Humbly, lovingly, gently, remember him, for he wants stillness for you and quiet."

Finding time for a sacred pause is not a luxury but a necessity. The length of time will depend on one's circumstances and season in life. Tersteegen—who set up a school for children in poverty, dispensed homemade medicines for the sick, corresponded with many people, wrote books of catechism and doctrine, and often had twenty or thirty people waiting to speak with him in the evenings—must have had a hard time finding stillness. But stillness, like solitude and silence, becomes a spiritual discipline.

Creating stillness—even if it's for just one minute—requires a conscious effort. "Guard your peace. Nothing is worth your disturbance," Tersteegen states. Taking a pause from the whirling activity to be still, as the psalmist advises, allows us to calm down and quiet our thoughts.

"My mind belongs in the house of God," Tersteegen acknowledges, "therefore it turns everything else away." Once we have learned the discipline of stillness in smaller increments, we can lengthen it. Eventually we will be able to sing along with Tersteegen, "Have peace in me that I may rest in you."

Be still and know that I am God,
Be still and know that I Am,
Be still and know,
Be still,
Be.

be still, and the heart will be put in harmony with God
GERhard TERSTEEGEN

Study to shew thyself approved unto God, a workman that needeth not to be ashamed, rightly dividing the word of truth.

—2 Timothy 2:15 KJV

Learning and gaining knowledge can be significant aspects of faith. To "have the mind of Christ," as Paul writes in 1 Corinthians 2:16, requires study, among other things. Our beliefs, when applied to our actions, become our faith.

Alcuin was a student of Scripture and world literature. Alcuin was "the most learned man anywhere to be found," wrote Einhard in his book *The Life of Charlemagne*. During his life, he became one of the catalysts for a surge in learning—what became known as the Carolingian Renaissance. During this period, there was an increase in literature and writing, an expansion of the visual arts and architecture, and an emphasis on liturgical reforms and scriptural studies.

Combining his interests in literature and art, Alcuin developed the script known today as the Carolingian minuscule font. The Carolingian script has been instrumental in English, providing a means for both upper and lowercase lettering. His leadership in the scriptorium—a room set aside in the monastery for the writing and copying of books—brought an increase in literature output and access to the scriptures to more people.

But Alcuin also understood that faith is a decision of the heart, not just the head. He implored Charlemagne to do away with the idea that conversion happens at the tip of the sword. Much of Christianity remained plagued by this barbaric act of forcing people to convert, which made its way to the Americas centuries later.

How we study is as important as what we read, and humility is essential. "What would it profit you if you knew the whole Bible by heart and the sayings of all the philosophers, but you never experienced the grace and love of God?" Thomas à Kempis writes. "Read humbly, simply, and faithfully, and do not seek a reputation for being learned."

Alcuin was a level-headed person whose study brought him into a deep knowledge of God.

Wonderful Counselor, may I never fear to seek truth. Bring wisdom and knowledge and guide my studies in your word and spiritual reading. Open doors and illuminate darkened rooms, revealing your glory. Amen.

IRRIGATE THEIR LANDS WITH LEARNING
ALCUIN OF YORK

For just as we share abundantly in the sufferings of Christ, so also our comfort abounds through Christ.

—2 CORINTHIANS 1:5

Suffering comes to all. There's no need to seek it out. But how we navigate challenging times can either place us in survival mode or draw us toward God. Saint Paul states, "We also glory in our sufferings, because we know that suffering produces perseverance; perseverance, character; and character, hope" (Rom 5:3–4).

The medieval mystic Catherine of Siena had a vision in which Jesus offered her two crowns: one made of gold, representing material wealth in this life, and one of thorns, for eternal riches. She chose the latter.

Catherine often visited the sick and the poor. She ran not away from suffering but toward it. She lived quietly, and she sometimes gave away her family's clothing and food to those in need—all without asking her family! Her life would be defined by suffering but also by joy. Like Christ, she died at age thirty-three.

Paul writes that "our present sufferings are not worth comparing with the glory that will be revealed in us" (Rom 8:18). A woman in labor suffers pain, but when the baby comes, her joy is complete. All the pain she experienced quickly fades; this is the hope and joy Paul alludes to as we endure suffering. Our pain, somehow, is bringing about transformation. We groan, along with all of nature, for this process to take place.

"Nothing great is ever achieved without much enduring," Catherine of Siena counsels. Like athletes training for a marathon, we press on and endure. "Run in such a way as to get the prize," Paul encourages us (1 Cor 9:24). Hope and joy are within our grasp. The crown of glory awaits.

Man of Sorrows, suffering is all around us. Sometimes the pain is more than I can endure. But if I have to be in this pain, may it count for eternity and greater intimacy with you. I pray with St. Catherine, "You are like a deep sea, in which the more I seek, the more I find; and the more I find, the more eagerly I seek." Amen.

INFLAME
ME WITH YOUR LOVE
catherine
of siena

Submit yourselves, then, to God. —James 4:7

Augustine, the son of a devout, praying mother, came to faith at age thirty-one. The North African philosopher describes this event in his autobiography, *Confessions*. Sitting in a garden, he heard a child singing a song, "Take up and read, take up and read." The Scriptures on the bench beside him had been blown open, and he grabbed the book. It was St. Paul's letter to the Romans, and he began reading: "Not in carousing and drunkenness, not in sexual immorality and debauchery, not in dissension and jealousy. Rather, clothe yourselves with the Lord Jesus Christ, and do not think about how to gratify the desires of the flesh" (Rom 13:13–14).

This was a powerful word for him for this season of his life. Augustine left the garden a changed man, with a new course of direction.

It would not be an easy surrender for the future saint and bishop of Hippo, as his *Confessions* testifies. Augustine became torn: between what he might have to give up, and what his life in Christ would mean. Was he ready to exchange a life of pleasure for a life of discipline, as he saw it? Was God's love truly sufficient?

When we discover that the Creator and Lover of our souls wants what's best for us, it becomes easier to relinquish our tight grip of control over our futures. Augustine succumbed. "Restless is our heart until it comes to rest in you," he would later write. He stepped into the unknown, the mystery of love, by his free will and by God's grace.

Surrendering his will would become a lifelong occupation. "I no longer placed any hope in this world," Augustine confessed, "but stood firmly upon the rule of faith."

O Most Merciful God, Lover of my soul, whatever is contrary to your purposes—for love and life, for health and healing, for fulfillment and joy, for that which you've created me to be—I surrender all! Amen.

LOVE IS THE BEAUTY OF THE SOUL
SAINT
AUGUSTINE

Accept one another, then, just as Christ accepted you, in order to bring praise to God. For I tell you that Christ has become a servant.

—Romans 15:7–8

The son of an aristocratic French family, Charles de Foucauld served in many positions—including as a soldier—until a radical conversion at twenty-eight years old. From that time forth, he set off to follow in the footsteps of Christ.

He did this quite literally, even living in Nazareth for a time. In subsequent years, he became a Trappist monk, a priest, and a hermit.

Hearing the words of Christ—"Truly, I say to you, as you did it to one of the least of these my brethren, you did it to me"—convinced Charles to relocate to Algeria, in the Sahara Desert, in 1900. Thus began his relationship with the nomadic Tuareg people.

Charles was aware of the differences between himself and the Tuareg. But he was also aware of the similarities. God had created all people, and Jesus had openly accepted all. His love has no qualifications. The dictionary defines tolerance as "sympathy or indulgence for beliefs or practices differing from or conflicting with one's own." Charles's mindset of tolerance—of *us* rather than *us* and *them*—allowed him to be accepted as a holy man by the Islamic Tuareg.

"Foucauld's originality lay in recognizing that it is not necessary to teach others, to cure them or to improve them," writes the *National Catholic Reporter*'s Kate White. "It is only necessary to live among them, sharing the human condition and being present to them in love."

Charles's life in the desert only brought him closer to God, closer to inner peace, and closer to those he served. When we are present to others in love, we practice tolerance—and not in the sense of merely putting up with them in a grudging way but in the sharing of the human condition. Jesus challenges us not to just tolerate others but to love them as he has loved us.

Compassionate One, I abandon my life to you. Let me carry Christ to others: not to "fix them," not to make them more like me, but simply to share your love and blessings with them. Amen.

Father of mine, I abandon myself to you
CHARLES DE FOUCAULD

But I am like an olive tree flourishing in the house of God; I trust in God's unfailing love for ever and ever.

—Psalm 52:8

Takashi Nagai's life changed abruptly on August 9, 1945, at 11:02 a.m. An atomic bomb exploded in Nagasaki, roughly 550 yards above the Urakami Cathedral, which had stood in an area occupied by Christian believers since the seventeenth century. The cathedral was destroyed, and dozens of priests and worshippers died instantly. In Nagasaki, forty thousand civilians were incinerated, with forty thousand more dying afterward from injuries or radiation complications.

Dr. Nagai found his wife's ashes where the kitchen of his home used to be. All that was left was part of her hand clutching her rosary. "Not only my present but also my past and future were blown away in the blast," Nagai writes. "My beloved students burned together in a ball of fire right before my eyes. Then I collected my wife . . . a bucket-full of soft ashes, from the burnt-out ruins of our house."

In the years following, Nagai built a small hermitage for prayer, painting, and writing: Nyokodo (Place of Love to Yourself Hermitage)—named after Nyoko Aijin (Love Your Neighbor as Yourself). The small shack was barely large enough to place a mattress, but Nagai would spend his remaining five years inside, bedridden.

Trying to make some sense of the horror and suffering, he did not abandon his faith or blame God. "Our church of Nagasaki kept the faith," Nagai writes. "During the war, this same church never ceased to pray day and night for lasting peace."

Nagai trusted that, although life is fleeting, the love of the Creator is universal, expanding, and ever eternal. He concludes, "Love everyone and trust his Providence, and you will find peace. I have tried it and can assure you it is so."

Prince of Peace, penetrate cold hearts that quickly turn to war. Bring protection and comfort to victims of war. Help us to trust you. Prepare within our hearts our own sanctuary that welcomes the stranger. Amen.

LOVE EVERYONE & TRUST HIS PROVIDENCE AND YOU WILL FIND PEACE.
永井隆
TAKASHI NAGAI

IDA B. WELLS (1862–1931) Truth

Love does not delight in evil but rejoices with the truth.

—1 Corinthians 13:6

Long before Rosa Parks chose to remain seated on the bus, Ida B. Wells did likewise in a train car. Both women challenged the same unjust system.

In 1884, Wells was asked by the conductor of the Chesapeake & Ohio Railroad Company to move from her first-class car seat—for which she had a ticket— to the Jim Crow section of the train. She refused, and she was subsequently forcibly removed. Under the Civil Rights Act of 1875, Wells filed and won a lawsuit against the company. Although she was awarded a settlement, not surprisingly, the verdict was appealed and reversed by the Tennessee Supreme Court.

This incident, followed by the lynching of three friends, set Wells on a course to seek social justice and stop anti-Black violence. She began her career as a prominent journalist by writing church editorials exposing racial injustice. Her prophetic voice empathized with the oppressed; it exposed lies, confronted evils, and appealed for transformation. "There must always be a remedy for wrong and injustice if we only know how to find it," Wells claims.

Activism became a natural extension of her contemplative life. Without God, there would be no change. "I do not fear," Wells writes in her diary. "God is over all and He will, so long as I am in the right, fight my battles and give me what is my right."

Ida B. Wells became a founding member of the National Association for the Advancement of Colored People in 1909. This community effort paved the way for the civil rights movement. Her passionate work to stop lynchings—along with that of Mamie Till and others—was finally realized on March 29, 2022, when the Emmett Till Antilynching Act made lynching a federal hate crime.

Ida B. Wells found remedies for wrong and injustice. She exposed lies and revealed truth.

God of Truth, expose the evils of injustice. Bring healing to the victims and families of such atrocities. Help me lend my voice to others who are seeking to remedy wrongs; hear our cry. Amen.

the way
to Right wrongs
is to turn the light
of truth upon them
~Ida B. Wells

FRANÇOIS FÉNELON (1651–1715) Unity

The kingdom of heaven is like a mustard seed, which a man took and planted in his field. Though it is the smallest of all seeds, yet when it grows, it is the largest of garden plants and becomes a tree, so that the birds come and perch in its branches.

—Matthew 13:31–32

Jesus's disciples couldn't accept his teaching about the mustard tree, with its celebration of the small and insignificant. They wanted a messiah of political power! But that isn't the kingdom this Messiah preached. Love your enemies, pray for those who persecute you, go the extra mile: Jesus offered his followers this pathway, an alternative to religious nationalism.

Seventeenth-century mystic François Fénelon lived in close proximity to power and knew that a national agenda would always seek its own interests. Fénelon was the spiritual director to a French duke and duchess, and later he became the personal tutor to the king's grandson. It was during this time that Fénelon wrote *The Adventures of Telemachus*, a novel denouncing war and mercantilism. "All wars are civil wars . . . 'tis still mankind shedding each others' blood," writes Fénelon elsewhere.

As the mustard tree puts out branches across borders of all kinds, the line between what divides us begins to dissolve—or rather it could, if we let it. Jesus's vision of a mustard tree offers a place where others can find peace and acceptance and safety. Fénelon agreed with the larger picture, stating, "Each individual owes incomparably more to the human race . . . than to the particular country in which he was born."

Is it possible to relinquish national idolatry? Fénelon offers us this advice: "Our devotion to God must never stop. We must put it into practice everywhere—in things we do not like, in things that disturb us, in things that go against our point of view, our inclinations, our plans. . . . To be willing to give of ourselves in this way, and to accept the consequences, is to be truly devout."

Jesus, you acted according to your Father's will, and you ask us, your disciples, to do the same. Pray in me and through me now. You exhibited love for all, and I pledge my allegiance to you. Amen.

may you yourself pray in me and through me
Francois Fenelon

The Son is the image of the invisible God. —COLOSSIANS 1:15

What might it mean to see the world in a sacred way? For centuries, monks in scriptoriums painstakingly copied illuminated prayer books. This meant these psalters were expensive, affordable only for the wealthy. Johannes Gutenberg's discovery of the printing press in 1440 would change all that. And no one took advantage of it more than northern German printmaker Albrecht Dürer.

Dürer returned from studying in Italy with new insights into perspective and chiaroscuro shading, incorporating both. These were cutting-edge ideas at the time. Dürer was also the first artist to use multiple vanishing points. His *Small Passion*, featuring thirty-six woodcuts on the life, death, and resurrection of Christ, became a bestseller. The initial publication in 1511 had accompanying religious poetry, but the book could be experienced by visuals alone. And for a largely illiterate population, this was an important feature.

Visio divina, or "divine vision," is a way of looking at an image with the intention of encountering God. To see in a sacred way, the Carthusian monk Ludolph of Saxony suggested the viewer look with compassion, admiration, exultation, imitation, and contemplation.

"Our experience of the divine is tremendously limited when we engage with Scriptures merely by means of intellectual understanding and belief," writes Juliet Benner in *Contemplative Vision*. Art, like music, initially bypasses our left-brained analytical side. We see lines, shapes, textures, and colors, and we have an immediate, visceral reaction. It's only after that initial encounter that we begin to analyze what we see. In addition, art speaks beyond language. Two people speaking different languages can "read" the same scene.

Dürer's *Small Passion* consists of artwork conducive to reflection, which naturally leads us to meditation. We "participate with the artist to see and experience God," writes Benner, in unique ways that we may not have considered. Dürer offers us something that is beyond communication through words alone.

O Divine Vision, Beautiful One, engage me in new and exciting ways, with the heart, mind, body, soul, senses, and imagination. Help me to recognize your voice in all things sacred. Help me to envision you and your creation. Amen.

HELP US TO RECOGNIZE YOUR VOICE
ALBRECHT DÜRER

Establish the work of our hands for us—
yes, establish the work of our hands.

—Psalm 90:17

What would it look like to offer up our work to God? Many of us long for fulfilling work. We long for God to "establish the work of our hands," as the psalmist writes. The Hebrew word for *establish* literally means to fix "a house upon pillars." What an excellent illustration: God is the foundation, and the work we do builds upon that foundation and enables us to serve others.

"The place God calls you to is the place where your deep gladness and the world's deep hunger meet," Frederick Buechner famously writes. The Presbyterian minister was also a Pulitzer Prize–nominated author. Throughout his long life, he penned thirty-nine books: novels, theological meditations, and memoirs.

It was in high school that Buechner found his passion to write. After graduating from Princeton, Buechner combined his writing talent with his desire to preach. He knew that our vocation was more than a job. Finding our purpose, educating ourselves, and being trained and equipped is a lifetime pursuit.

Whether our work is fulfilling or unfulfilling, seeing our jobs as actually serving Christ can bring greater clarity and purpose. Throughout our lifetime, we will almost certainly have jobs we like and dislike; some we'll have to step away from, and others we might lose. God uses each season to direct us, to shine and buff the diamonds we are. We can serve God's purposes even if we find ourselves in a dead-end job.

Our vocation isn't necessarily our dream job or some destination we spend our whole lives reaching. Our vocation lies in living in Christ daily. *How* we do is as important as *what* we do.

What needs of the world do you fulfill? Where do you find your joy? Buechner would remind us that our vocation needn't be grandiose. With talent, desire, and dedication, do your work wholeheartedly, and know that God's favor rests on you!

Giver of all good gifts, you've equipped me with special talents, unique insights, desires, and dreams. I have something to offer others through my vocation. Help me to go where you take me. Amen.

GO WHERE YOUR BEST PRAYERS TAKE YOU
F. Buechner

You heard my cry for mercy when I called to you for help.

—PSALM 31:22

Francis was kneeling before a crucifix in a small, dilapidated chapel when he first experienced Christ on a mystical level. "Rebuild my church!" were the words he heard from the icon, and so he quickly got to work replacing every stone and beam that needed repair. But Francis soon realized the repair the church needed wasn't about material construction but spiritual renewal.

One day, while riding his horse in the valley outside the city walls of Assisi, Francis came upon a person with leprosy begging for bread. Francis's first biographer, Peter of Celano, tells us that Francis was terrified of leprosy. But in the spur of the moment, Francis dismounted his horse, ran to the surprised leper, and gave him money and a kiss.

"What had seemed bitter to me was turned into sweetness of soul and body," Francis says. It was an early stage in Francis's spiritual journey. But from that day forth, he would embrace and serve those living in the leper colony. Those who had initially repulsed him became good, trusted friends.

Francis is well-known for his intuitive connections to and love for the creatures of the natural world. He saw God being praised through Brother Son and Sister Moon, and he has become the patron saint of ecologists.

Francis also miraculously received the stigmata, wounds of the crucified Christ, at the end of his life. He had learned to relinquish his pride, embrace poverty, and become vulnerable enough to humble himself to all.

In that hazy area between misery and mercy, between God's good grace and human effort, healing finds a home. By becoming vulnerable, we, like Francis, can give and accept love.

Mighty Healer, I walk among those different than me, and I might not understand them. Help me to see beyond the exterior and understand this: all hearts need love and compassion. Your Spirit strengthens me in my weakness so I might face my fears with courage and love. Amen.

PRAISED BE YOU MY LORD WITH ALL YOUR CREATURES ESPECIALLY BROTHER SUN
Francis of Assisi

But if we hope for what we do not yet have, we wait for it patiently.

—Romans 8:25

English poet Christina Rossetti wrote one of the most beloved Christmas poems of the Victorian era, "A Christmas Carol," in 1872. Composer Gustav Holst set it to music thirty-one years later as the hymn "In the Bleak Midwinter."

In the poem, Rossetti paints a picture of the waiting leading up to the Christ child's appearance in Bethlehem. The ground is cold and icy—"Earth stood hard as iron / Water like a stone." We can feel the bite of the cold wind on our cheeks; the "frosty wind made moan." Perhaps Rossetti is describing our hearts. Or maybe she was thinking of the desperate situation of the women who were leaving prostitution—those being ministered to at St. Mary of Magdalene House of Charity, where she volunteered.

Waiting is a part of our daily lives. We wait at the traffic light and for the "next representative" on the phone. We await God's direction, healing, and answers. Advent, the season of the church calendar that precedes Christmas, is all about waiting. "We wait for the blessed hope—the appearing of the glory of our great God and Savior, Jesus Christ," St. Paul writes (Titus 2:13).

In Rossetti's poem, the divine merges with the banal—cherubim, seraphim, and archangels mix with "ox and ass and camel." The stable and hay are made holy: a sacred place, set apart and suitable for what will be revealed. Finally, in the last stanza and a half, the wait is over. The promise has arrived. The young maiden Mary worships Jesus with a kiss.

And the poet? How does she worship? She would undoubtedly offer a lamb, she writes—if she were a shepherd. She would offer expensive gifts from the East—if she were a wise man. But her hands are empty.

We, like Rossetti, often feel we have little to offer. We feel like life is mostly waiting for something to happen. But even as we wait, like the poet, we can give to the Christ child our hearts.

Christ of wonder, we await your coming and your return again. Enlighten me, and implant a hope to sustain my heart, a heart given fully to you and the mystery that is revealed. Amen.

enlighten us, thou who art fire of love
Christina Rossetti

For we were all baptized by one Spirit so as to form one body—whether Jews or Gentiles, slave or free—and we were all given the one Spirit to drink.

—1 Corinthians 12:13

Isabella Bomfree was born into slavery in 1797 in rural New York. Separated from her family at age nine, she was purchased and sold several times. When she chose to follow the way of Christ in 1843, the first thing she did was change her name to Sojourner Truth. From then on, she boldly up and walked to freedom as an itinerant preacher, sharing the gospel and advocating for abolition and women's suffrage. She admits, "I did not run off, for I thought that wicked, but I walked off, believing that to be all right." Sojourner worked tirelessly for those still enslaved and the marginalized.

Sojourner Truth crossed paths with the likes of Susan B. Anthony and Frederick Douglass. During one rally, Douglass called for a revolt against the system. When Sojourner Truth took the stage, she questioned Douglass as to whether God had died. Her faith held fast to the sovereignty of God and the belief that God would ultimately address such injustice.

Sojourner Truth witnessed to the power of God, and she walked across all sorts of boundaries.

On one of Jesus's travels to Jerusalem, he deliberately chooses to walk through Samaria, a region where he doesn't "belong." Thirsty from the long walk, Jesus stops to get a drink at a well where a Samaritan woman is drawing water. He engages in conversation—a cultural faux pas at the time—in broad daylight. And the friendly exchange deals with sharing—may I have something you have? I might have something for you!

Like Jesus's disciples, who were baffled by his audacity, we can acclimate ourselves to harmful ideologies and racism. But from Sojourner Truth, we can learn how to walk toward freedom.

Is God gone? If our answer is no, we can witness to the power of God.

Light of lights, send me out to brighten the world, to witness to the truth, and mirror your mercy. Amen.

I will not allow my life's light to be determined by the darkness around me
Sojourner Truth

Look at the birds of the air. . . . See how the flowers of the field grow.

—MATTHEW 6:26, 28

A sense of wonder defined the life of George Washington Carver, one of America's most outstanding agricultural scientists. "I love to think of nature as an unlimited broadcasting station," he says, "through which God speaks to us every hour if we will only tune in."

From playing in the backwoods of Missouri as a child, he experienced what Rabbi Abraham Joshua Heschel referred to as "radical amazement." "Get up in the morning and look around at the world in a way that takes nothing for granted," Heschel said.

Carver did just that! Often rising at 4:30 in the morning, he would wander into the woods. "I was practically overwhelmed with a sense of some Great Presence," Carver writes. "Not only had someone been there [in the woods], someone was there. . . . Never since have I been without this consciousness of the Creator speaking to me."

Born into slavery, Carver went to school in an era in which it was rare for schools to accept Black students. One of his teachers noticed his plant drawings and encouraged him to pursue botany. Another told him, "You must learn all you can, then go back out into the world and give your learning back to the people."

Young George took this to heart. He received his master's degree in 1896, and after a short stint elsewhere, Carver taught and did research at the Tuskegee Institute. He discovered over three hundred uses for the peanut, and he encouraged the use of crop rotation to enrich depleted soil. Carver's discoveries proved beneficial for Southern farmers' way of life.

Driven by his love for God and neighbor, Carver states, "As I worked on projects which fulfilled a real human need, forces were working through me, which amazed me. I would often go to sleep with an insoluble problem. When I woke, the answer was there."

O Beautiful One, who causes fauna and flora to flourish: take my offerings and multiply them. Increase my sense of wonder and radical amazement at you and the world you created. Amen.

my
purpose
alone
must
be
God's
purpose

Sing to the Lord a new song. —Psalm 96:1

Thea Bowman grew up in the Jim Crow South, in Canton, Mississippi. Education for Black children was limited. But opportunities for her changed when the Catholic Church sent four nuns to begin a school exclusively for Black children.

Young Thea saw something different in these women. They were not knuckle-slapping white ladies. Rather, they tenderly held Black babies and respectfully addressed her mother as "Mrs. Bowman" rather than "girl," as the other white women had. If the sisters initially showed Bowman the love of the living Christ, then in return, she offered them lessons in the beauty, vibrancy, and praise of the African diaspora.

At age fifteen, Thea became the first African American member of the convent in La Crosse, Wisconsin, where she addressed racism within the church using symbolic gestures. "We don't want to change the sacraments," she later said. "We don't want to change the theology of the church. We just want to express that theology within the roots of our Afro-centric spiritual culture."

Music played a vital role in her spirituality. Thea began every class and speaking engagement with songs dear to her heart. With her operatic voice and background choir, Bowman would eventually record two albums. She also collected songs for a hymnal to represent music and oral tradition in Black faith. *Lead Me, Guide Me: The African American Catholic Hymnal* was the first such work directed to the Black community.

Bowman's work was not without backlash. People had told her that her Black expressions of music and worship were "un-Catholic." In one speaking engagement, Bowman addressed the bishops by starting off singing the Black spiritual "Sometimes I Feel Like a Motherless Child." She concluded her speech by pleading, "Can you hear me, Church . . . Will you help me? Jesus told me the Church is my home."

For us, like Thea, worship can embody faith and give it voice.

Divine Conductor, orchestrate your songs of praise. Blend each of us as a unique instrument into a beautiful symphony of harmonious sound. Amen.

Thea
Bowman
Remember who
you are & whose
you are

JOHN BAILLIE (1886–1960) Written Prayer

Go now, write it on a tablet for them, inscribe it on a scroll, that for the days to come it may be an everlasting witness.

—Isaiah 30:8

The Psalms are some of the earliest examples of written prayer. Writing our prayers can offer us something that speaking our prayers cannot. Slowing down to consider and select each word carefully, we create an interlude for meditation. In that moment of silence, we allow ourselves to be a receiver of the Divine.

John Baillie was a Scottish theologian who taught at Inverness Royal Academy, Auburn Theological Seminary, and Union Theological Seminary. In 1936, a collection of sixty-two of his prayers became the book *A Diary of Private Prayer.* Now considered a devotional classic, it offers morning and evening prayers for one month. "Eternal Father of my soul, let my first thought today be of You," Baillie begins, on day 1.

Besides forcing us to slow down, written prayer has another advantage. Writing our prayers, like journaling, allows us to recall times, events, and people we've interceded for. Prayers carry a prophetic quality, and our faith strengthens when we return to a prayer we have seen answered.

Baillie's prayers have depth and richness. He doesn't just stick to a formula. Some days he begins with praise or thanksgiving; other days he requests guidance and direction. He prays for himself, friends and family, the church, and the world.

"May my love for other people grow deeper and more tender, and may I be more willing to take their burdens upon myself," John Baillie writes. "To your care, O God, I commend my soul and the souls of all whom I love and who love me."

We can offer up all things to God, and writing our prayers can provide an everlasting witness to God's faithfulness.

Living Word, may my prayers offer praise and thanksgiving. Write your commandments on my heart even as I write my prayers to you. In all things, help my words to reflect truth and honesty. Amen.

ETERNAL FATHER OF MY SOUL, LET MY FIRST THOUGHT TODAY BE OF YOU
JOHN BAILLIE

The virgin will conceive and give birth to a son, and will call him Immanuel.

—Isaiah 7:14

Tradition has it that Saint Luke, the Gospel writer, painted the first Madonna and Child icon. The simple double portrait has been depicted in many ways ever since, known by the Greek names of *Theotokos*, *Eleousa*, *Paraclesis*, or *Hodegetria*, among others. The *Eleousa* icon shows a close, intimate cheek-to-cheek representation, while the *Hodegetria* [Black Madonna of Częstochowa, illustrated here] has Mary pointing to her Son as the way of salvation.

Icons are an essential connection with God for Orthodox Christians. One observer calls them "a window into the heavenly world." As the *word* communicates, so does the *image*. Whether we take in information about God through our ears or eyes, our ultimate objective is to engage in heartfelt interaction. We can meditate on an icon or simply rest with it as we gaze at its beauty.

For those unfamiliar with this art form: the icon does not pretend to depict a realistic representation of God. As such, it's not idolatry. An icon is a symbolic tool. Like the metaphorical, poetic language of the Psalms, an icon can help us grasp the character of God. The artist "writes" the icon in colors, shapes, lines, and patterns, and what unfolds before our eyes is something relatable, something we can understand, something that bridges the gap between physical and spiritual, between human and divine.

This is what the *Hodegetria* icon represents: God is with us and is now in us. God in the flesh. The intimacy of God's love is depicted here before us. "For God so loved the world that he gave his one and only Son," John tells us. "For God did not send his Son into the world to condemn the world, but to save the world through him" (John 3:16–17).

During Advent, this icon can be a part of your devotional reading. Return to it often. Let Mary point you on the way of salvation. Let yourself gaze in awe and wonder on the Incarnate Christ.

O Indwelling Presence, may my eyes behold your beauty: the Divine One who entered time from eternity, humanity through Mary, and lives in me now. Amen.

HODEGETRIA

"I am the Alpha and the Omega," says the Lord God, "who is, and who was, and who is to come, the Almighty."

—Revelation 1:8

Jesus Christ, Pantocrator: Lord of the Universe, Almighty, Ruler of all. The *Pantocrator* icon is considered one of the oldest Byzantine icons of the Savior. The initial iconographer wrote in the image what St. John painted in words: "The Word was God. . . . The Word became flesh and made his dwelling among us" (John 1:1, 14).

During the fourth century, people of Christian faith struggled against heresies concerning Christ's divinity and humanity. Saint Athanasius remained steadfast to St. John's gospel theology and opposed these attacks. The Nicene Creed, written in the year 325, would lay down the tenets of the faith, affirming that "Christ was the visible and perfect image of the Father."

The members of the council that created the creed recorded that Christ was "true God from true God, begotten, not made, consubstantial with the Father; through him all things were made." *Consubstantial* means "of the same substance." Christ was begotten, unlike us, who are created.

The iconographer presents this dualistic nature of Christ—God and human—by painting a human side and an "otherworldly" half. It is subtle, but it's there nonetheless. Christ holds the Gospels in one hand while blessing the viewer with the other. His eyes pierce our soul. They look longingly and lovingly at us. We are his beloved, loved from the foundation of the world! There is nothing he wouldn't do so as to never be separated from us.

"The Cross of the Lord is a sign of victory over death," Athanasius reminds us. Look on the victorious Christ in all his glory, and hear his words: "I am the resurrection." Christ has defeated death. He is risen! He is risen indeed!

The Lord bless you and keep you, the Lord make his face shine upon you . . . the Lord turn his face toward you and give you peace. In the name of the Father, the Son, and the Holy Spirit, Amen.

IC
XC

Reading Guides

The liturgical calendar marks the dates of Christmas and Easter celebrations and the preliminary fasting days known as Advent and Lent. Advent, in Western Christianity, begins the fourth Sunday before Christmas (22 to 28 days), while in Eastern Christianity (Eastern Catholic Churches and Eastern Orthodox churches), the Nativity Fast begins on November 15 (40 days), ending on December 24.

Lent always begins on Ash Wednesday in the West—Clean Monday for Great Lent in the East—and is the forty-six days leading up to Easter, not including Sundays, making it forty days long (forty continuous days in Eastern Christianity). The time for Lent will vary as Easter coincides with the first Sunday after the Paschal Full Moon. Lent was initially observed in the late third or early fourth century, while Advent was first practiced in the late fifth century.

Advent and Lent are times of remembrance, waiting, and expectant hope, all occurring simultaneously. Christ came; Christ is here; Christ is coming.

The following lists feature forty-one devotional readings for each observance and two traditional Orthodox icons for your *visio divina* meditation. I'd encourage you to sit still with them often. While the lists can be interchangeable, the Advent meditations focus more specifically on the mystery of the incarnation, Christ taking on human flesh—the inward, contemplative life. The Lenten devotions focus on the outward, active life—Christ moving out among the people: feeding, healing, and bringing resurrected life.

We enter the liturgical seasons with an artist's eye—the eye of our imagination.

ADVENT

Saddle up your camels, for in the morning we travel to the little town of Bethlehem. Each day we will move closer to the wonder we seek—the Christ child. He is the Prince of Peace, Immanuel—God is with us. He is our hope of glory!

Our companions for this journey are the wise men and wise women: the saints and mystics who have traveled this terrain before us. While we traverse the desert sands, Amma Syncletica will guide us. She knows of the *endurance* it will take. And Amma Theodora will instruct us on *resilience*. Our prayer life will expand with the insights of the Pilgrim and Brother Lawrence—God is always near, closer than our breath. Drawing near to the manger, we will humbly *worship* and *praise* in hushed tones with Sister Thea Bowman and Jacopone da Todi.

ADVENT—The Contemplative Life

(November 15 to December 25)

Week I. Preparation (Nov. 15)

1. Mary of Egypt—Repentance
2. Jean-Pierre de Caussade—Presence
3. Guigo II—*Lectio Divina*
4. Albrecht Durer—*Visio Divina*

Week II. Mystery (Nov. 19)

5. Meister Eckhart—Silence
6. Geerhard Tersteegen—Stillness
7. Cloud of Unknowing (Anonymous)—Contemplation
8. Ignatius of Loyola—Imagination
9. George Washington Carver—Wonder
10. Hildegard of Bingen—Creativity

Week III. The Desert (Nov. 25)

11. Abba Macarius—Selflessness
12. Amma Theodora—Resilience
13. Amma Syncletica—Endurance
14. Abba Antony—Spiritual Warfare
15. Abba Moses—Intimacy
16. Abba Joseph—Passion

Week IV. Prayer (Dec. 1)

17. Martin Luther—Rule of Prayer
18. The Pilgrim—Jesus Prayer
19. John Baillie—Written Prayer
20. Jeanne Guyon—Praying Scripture
21. Romuald—Fixed-Hour Prayer
22. Brother Lawrence—Unceasing Prayer

Week V. Individual Praxis (Dec. 7)

23. Victor-Antoine D'Avila-Latourrette—Rhythm of Life
24. Benedict of Nursia—Humility
25. Clare of Assisi—Simplicity
26. Augustine of Hippo—Surrender
27. Seraphim of Sarov—Solitude
28. Ambrose of Milan—Rest

Week VI. Community Praxis (Dec. 13)

29. François Fénelon—Unity
30. Clarence Jordan—Fellowship
31. Eileen Egan—Gospel Nonviolence

32. Mechthild of Magdeburg—Compassion
33. Frederick Buechner—Vocation
34. Charles de Foucauld—Tolerance

Week VII. Celebration (Dec. 19)

35. Origin Adamantius—Christocentrism
36. Christina Rossetti—Waiting
37. Nicholas of Myra—Generosity
38. Thea Bowman—Worship
39. C. S. Lewis—Joy
40. Jacopone da Todi—Praise

CHRISTMAS: Mother Mary and Child (*Hodegetria*)—Incarnation

LENT

We board the vessel that will sail to our pilgrimage destination: Jerusalem. The Celtic saints—Columba and Brendan—are accomplished wayfaring companions. We join them in the *mystery* that is to come. Once on solid ground, we are met by Takashi Nagai, who instructs us on how to *trust*. We are challenged by other witnesses of God's grace: Harriet Tubman, who embodies *perseverance*; Mother Teresa, sharing a life of *servanthood*; and Rosa Parks, inspiring us with her *courage*.

Gathering together, we earnestly pray with Jesus in the garden of his suffering. We relinquish our false selves by fasting and offering alms—acts of love, peace, generosity, and justice. Along with Perpetua, Felicitas, and Simon of Cyrene, we carry our cross up Golgotha to the place of Christ's death—the place of our death.

But on Easter morning, as the first sun's rays peer over the horizon, the comforting words of John Chrysostom ring out: "Christ is risen and the angels rejoice. Christ is risen and life is freed. Christ is risen and the tomb is emptied of the dead!"

Draw close to God during Lent—a time we can take inventory of our spiritual life. May you receive encouragement, instruction, and blessing from all the mystics and saints.

LENT—The Active Life

(Ash Wednesday to Easter, not including Sundays)

Week I. Preparing for the Journey (Ash Wednesday)

1. John the Baptist—Faith
2. Djan Darada—Baptism
3. Abba Poemen—Fasting
4. Thomas Merton—Journaling

Week II. Pilgrims and *Peregrini* (First Monday)

1. Columba of Iona—Pilgrimage
2. Patrick of Ireland—Forgiveness
3. Brigid of Kildare—Hospitality
4. Hilda of Whitby—Encouragement
5. Aidan of Lindisfarne—Gentleness
6. Brendan of Clonfert—Mystery

Week III. A Firm Foundation (Second Monday)

1. Desmond Tutu—Mercy
2. Harriett Tubman—Perseverance
3. Adolfo Pérez Esquivel—Hope
4. Wangari Maathai—Care for Creation
5. Francis of Assisi—Vulnerability
6. Black Elk—Kinship

Week IV. Servants of God (Third Monday)

1. Takashi Nagai—Trust
2. Sojourner Truth—Witness
3. Francis de Sales—Spiritual Formation
4. Sadhu Sundar Singh—Holiness
5. Josephine Bakhita—Freedom
6. John Wesley—Christian Perfection

Week V. Healing Hands (Fourth Monday)

1. John M. Perkins—Reconciliation
2. Martin de Porres—Healing
3. Mother Teresa—Servanthood
4. Aelred of Rievaulx—Soul Friendship
5. Henri Nouwen—Downward Mobility
6. Chief Seattle—Harmony

Week VI. Others Oriented (Fifth Monday)

1. Dorothy Day—Activism
2. Rosa Parks—Courage
3. Martin Luther King Jr.—Leadership
4. Ida B. Wells—Truth
5. Fannie Lou Hamer—Determination
6. Maurice Ouellet—Compassion

Week VII. Weapons of Love (Sixth Monday)

1. Perpetua and Felicitas—Loyalty
2. Corrie ten Boom—Solidarity
3. Dietrich Bonhoeffer—Community
4. Maximilian Kolbe—Love
5. Simon of Cyrene—Obedience
6. John Chrysostom—Resurrection

EASTER: Jesus Christ (*Pantocrator*)—Glory

Notes

Dorothy Day "There is plenty": Dorothy Day, *Loaves and Fishes* (San Francisco: Harper & Row, 1963), 210.

Satoko Kitahara "Vagrants sleeping": Paul Glynn, *The Smile of a Ragpicker: The Life of Satoko Kitahara* (San Francisco: Ignatius Press, 2014), 297.

Brother Lawrence All quotations come from Brother Lawrence, *The Practice of the Presence of God* (New York: Fleming H. Revell, 1895).

Wangari Maathai "We owe it to ourselves": Joseph Kabiru, "Farewell Wangari Maathai," *Guardian*, September 26, 2011; "malnutrition": Wangari Maathai, *Unbowed: A Memoir* (New York: Alfred A. Knopf, 2006); "Love Ourselves": Wangari Maathai, *Replenishing the Earth: Spiritual Values for Healing Ourselves and the World* (New York: Doubleday Religion, 2010).

John Wesley "Absolute perfection": John Wesley, *A Plain Account of Christian Perfection, 1766*; "By justification": John Wesley, journal (quoting a letter of June 27, 1769; *Works*, 22:191–92).

Origen Adamantius "The right way": Rowan A. Greer, *Origen: An Exhortation to Martyrdom; Prayer; First Principles: Book IV, Prologue to the Commentary on the Song of Songs; Homily XXVII on Numbers* (Mahwah, NJ: Paulist Press, 1979).

Dietrich Bonhoeffer All quotations come from Dietrich Bonhoeffer, *Life Together* (New York: Harper & Row, 1954).

Mechthild of Magdeburg All quotations from Carmen Acevedo Butcher, trans., *The Cloud of Unknowing* (Boston: Shambhala Publications, 2009).

Rosa Parks "Faith in God": Douglas Brinkley, *Rosa Parks: A Life* (New York: Penguin Books, 2000); "You must never": quoted in "You Fight, to Breathe Again," Journalism, Technology, and Democracy, July 6, 2019, http://tinyurl.com/4d8wets2; Jessica Mazzola, "Newark Home to State's First Rosa Parks Statue, Officials Say," NJ.com, http://tinyurl.com/r959fubv.

Hildegard of Bingen "The Word is living": St. Hildegard of Bingen, *Scivias*; "musical brilliance": *The Symphonia and Ordo Virtutum of Hildegard von Bingen*, Nathaniel M. Campbell, Beverly R. Lomer, and Xenia Sandstrom-McGuire, International Society of Hildegard von Bingen Studies. Hildegard-society.org.

Abba Macarius "Go to the seminary": Benedicta Ward, trans., *The Sayings of the Desert Fathers: The Alphabetical Collection* (Kalamazoo, MI: Cistercian Publications, 1975), 132; "As long as": Henri Nouwen, *Peacework: Prayer, Resistance, Community* (Maryknoll, NY: Orbis Books, 2005), 36.

Fannie Lou Hamer "Sick and tired": Fannie Lou Hamer, speech, Williams Institutional CME Church, Harlem, New York, December 20, 1964; "You can pray": Fannie Lou Hamer, speech, Indianola, Mississippi, September 1964; "Have a little talk": Rev. Cleavant Derricks, "Just a Little Talk with Jesus."

Pandita Ramabai Dongre-Medhavi "I realized": Pandita Ramabai, *The Pandita Ramabai Story: In Her Own Words* (Clinton, NJ: Mukti Mission US, 2019); "to promote education": Dr. Shayequa Tanzeel, *Pandita Ramabai Sarasvati*, DDU Gorkhpur University, http://tinyurl.com/3jspfshs.

John Climacus "Love, by its nature": Vassilios Papavassiliou. *Thirty Steps to Heaven: The Ladder of Divine Ascent for All Walks of Life* (Chesterton, IN: Ancient Faith Publishing, 2013), 126.

Henri Nouwen"Just as we came": Henri Nouwen, *The Selfless Way of Christ: Downward Mobility and the Spiritual Life* (Maryknoll, NY: Orbis Books, 2011).

Maurice Ouellet "While I am Bishop" and "It was haunting": quoted in Robert Howell, "45 Years after March, Selma Priest Remembers Bloody Sunday," CNN "In America," March 8, 2010, http://tinyurl.com/2w7yre63; "Her eyes focused" and "I wiped": Quoted in Maurice Ouellet, homily, *Summer in Selma* (blog) Summerinselma.blogspot.com, 2013.

Hilda of Whitby "Encouraged him": Rev. Brenda Warren, "St. Hilda of Whitby," *Godspace* (blog), November 17, 2016, http://tinyurl.com/2xwr5kd8; "Keep the peace": Bede, *Ecclesiastical History of England*, book IV, chap. XXIII, "Abbess Hilda of Whitby," seventh century.

Amma Syncletica "Those who put": Ward, *The Sayings of the Desert Fathers*, 233.

Jarena Lee "There seemed a voice": "Jarena Lee and the Early A.M.E. Church," National Museum of African American History and Culture, http://tinyurl.com/yprxtyu4.

Abba Poemen "I think it better": Ward, *The Sayings of the Desert Fathers*, 171; "The nature of water": Ward, *The Sayings of the Desert Fathers*, 192.

Clarence Jordan All quotations from Clarence Jordan, *The Inconvenient Gospel: A Southern Prophet Tackles War, Wealth, Race, and Religion* (Walden, NY: Plough Publishing House, 2002).

Josephine Bakhita "Is charged with": "Feast Day of St. Josephine Bakhita," Mother Cabrini.org, February 2, 2022, http://tinyurl.com/2dfbfbrw.

Aidan of Lindisfarne "Giving them the milk": Bede, *A History of the English Church and People*, trans. Leo Sherley-Price (London: Penguin Classics, 1955); "As the tide": Parish of Guiseley with Esholt, https://guiseleyandesholt.org.uk/.

Eileen Egan "Rejects war": "Our Vision," Pax Christi, https://paxchristiusa.org/about/our-vision/; "use the Eucharist": quoted in Judith Valente, *A Lesson from Peace Activist Eileen Egan in This Time of War*, February 27, 2022 https://judithvalente.medium.com/a-lesson-from-peace-activist-eileen-egan-in-this-time-of-war-861b16cff27d.

Thérèse of Lisieux "Jesus does not ask": Saint Therese of Lisieux, *Story of a Soul*, trans. Thomas Taylor (self-published, 2022), 152; "With me": Therese of Lisieux, *Story of a Soul*, 137; "Count your": Johnson Oatman, "Count Your Blessings," 1897.

Chief Seattle The words of Chief Seattle come from a later text of the speech using a playwright's literary reworking. See Rudolf Kaiser, "Chief Seattle's Speech(es): American Origins and European Reception," in *Recovering the Word: Essays on Native American Literature*, ed. Brian Swann and Arnold Krupat (Berkeley: University of California Press, 1987), 528.

Sadhu Sundar Singh "I have come": C. F. Andrews, *Sadhu Sundar Singh: A Personal Memoir* (London: Hodder & Stoughton Limited, 1934); "Someday": Kim Comer, *Wisdom of the Sadhu: Teachings of Sundar Singh* (East Sussex: Plough Publishing House, 2000); "where You are": Sadhu Sundar Singh, *At the Master's Feet*, trans. Rev. Arthur and Mrs. Parker (London: Fleming H. Revell, 1922).

Adolfo Pérez Esquivel "Colonization": David B. Gowler, "A Non-violent Battle for Justice," The Visual Commentary on Scripture, http://tinyurl.com/57bvx6se; "We live in hope": Adolfo Pérez Esquivel Acceptance Speech, The Nobel Prize website, http://tinyurl.com/ycwtf3uh.

Ignatius of Loyola "All the things": David L. Fleming, SJ, *A Contemporary Reading of the Spiritual Exercises: A Companion to St. Ignatius' Text*, 2nd ed. (Chestnut Hill, MA: Institute of Jesuit Sources, 1980).

Óscar Romero "We have never": Óscar Romero, Homily, November 27, 1977; "Peace is dynamism": Óscar Romero, *The Violence of Love*, comp. and trans. James R. Brockman SJ (Maryknoll, NY: Orbis Books, 2004), 41.

Howard Thurman "Sometimes in the stillness": Howard Thurman, *Meditations of the Heart* (Boston: Beacon Books, 2023), 66.

Abba Moses "Do not be": *Give Me a Word: The Alphabetical Sayings of the Desert Fathers*, trans. John Wortley (Yonkers, NY: St. Vladimir's Seminary Press, 2014), 198; "My sins are": Wortley, *Give Me a Word*, 194.

***The Way of the Pilgrim*, Anonymous** "Sit down": Anonymous, *The Way of a Pilgrim.*

Thomas Merton "I must put": Thomas Merton, *Run to the Mountain, September 1, 1949*, vol 1. (San Francisco: HarperOne, 1995); 365–66; "Merton saw": Merton, *Run to the Mountain*, September 1, 1949, 1:365–66; "To write is to think": Merton, September 27, 1958, *A Search for Solitude*, vol. 3, 219; "become true": Merton, *A Search for Solitude* , November 12, 1952, 24; "[live] out": Jonathan Montaldo, ed., *A Year with Thomas Merton: Daily Meditations from His Journals* (New York: Harper Collins, 2004), xi.

C. S. Lewis "If you want joy": C. S. Lewis, *Mere Christianity* (New York: Touchstone 1996), 153; "joy worth having": Lewis, *Mere Christianity*, 52.

Mamie Till All quotations from Mamie Till-Mobley and Christopher Benson, *Death of Innocence: The Story of the Hate Crime That Changed America* (New York: Random House, 2003).

Black Elk "I am connected": Thomas Constantine Maroukis, *Peyote and the Yankton Sioux: The Life and Times of Sam Necklace* (Norman: University of Oklahoma Press, 2005), 160; "The Earth": Black Elk and Joseph Epes Brown, *The Sacred Pipe: Black Elk's Account of the Seven Rites of the Oglala Sioux* (Norman: University of Oklahoma Press, 1989); "I have come": quoted in Kent Nerburn, *The Wisdom of the Native Americans* (Novato, CA: New World Library, 1999).

Martin Luther King Jr. "We've got to revolt": Martin Luther King Jr., *A Call to Conscience: The Landmark Speeches of Dr. Martin Luther King, Jr.*, ed. Claiborne Carson and Kris Shepard (New York: Hachette, 2001), 32; "Once, in Montgomery": King, *A Call to Conscience*, 90; "I just want": King, *A Call to Conscience*, 222.

Guigo II "Dialogue with the text": Michael Casey, *Sacred Reading: The Ancient Art of Lectio Divina* (Liguori, MO: Liguori/Triumph, 1995); "We abide": M. Basil Pennington, *Lectio Divina: Renewing the Ancient Practice of Praying the Scriptures* (New York: Cistercian Abbey of Spencer, 1998).

Maximilian Kolbe All quotations from Patricia Treece, *A Man for Others: Maximilian Kolbe the "Saint of Auschwitz"—in the Words of Those Who Knew Him* (New York: Harper & Row Publishers, 1982).

Perpetua and Felicitas "The Martyrdom of Perpetua and Felicitas," introductory notice of the translator Rev. R. E. Wallis, http://tinyurl.com/s254xfmd.

Desmond Tutu "When I forgive": "Archbishop Desmond Tutu," *Guardian*, December 26, 2021, http://tinyurl.com/3x22xt5z, 2:42; "I have no hope": quoted in Alan Cowell, "Tutu Urges More Sanctions against South Africa," *New York Times*, April 3, 1986; "Do your little bit" is attributed to Tutu.

Abba Joseph "If you will": Ward, *The Sayings of the Desert Fathers*, 103.

Harriet Tubman "It wasn't me": quoted in Sarah Hopkins Bradford, *Harriet, the Moses of Her People* (Floyd, VA: SMK Books, 2018), 26; "I looked at my hands": Bradford, *Harriet*, 14.

Jeanne Guyon All quotations are from Jeanne Guyon, *Experiencing the Depths of Jesus Christ*, ed. Gene Edwards (Goleta, CA: Christian Books, 1975).

Jean-Pierre de Caussade All quotations from Jean-Pierre de Caussade, *Abandonment to Divine Providence* except "All that is required": Susan Muto, *A Feast for Hungry Souls: Spiritual Lessons from the Church's Greatest Masters and Mystics* (Notre Dame, IN: Ave Maria Press, 2020), 258.

John M. Perkins "Almost immediately": John M. Perkins, *One Blood: Parting Words to the Church on Race and Love* (Chicago: Moody Publishers, 2018), 37; "This is a God-sized" and "It isn't that they": Perkins, *One Blood*, 16; "One of the most": Perkins, *One Blood*, 152–53.

Mary of Egypt "The young man": Bruce Marshall, *The World, the Flesh and Father Smith* (Boston: Houghton Mifflin Company, 1945).

Amma Theodora "Just as the trees": Ward, *The Sayings of the Desert Fathers*; "Resilient people": Justine Allain-Chapman, *The Resilient Disciple: A Lenten Journey from Adversity to Maturity* (London: SPCK, 2018).

Ambrose of Milan "We especially care": Joshua Abraham Heschel, *The Sabbath* (New York: Farrar Straus Giroux, 1951); "I look at [Christ]": Mother Teresa, *Heart of Joy*, ed. Jose Luis Gonzalez-Balado (Ann Arbor, MI: Servant Books, 1987), 135.

Victor-Antoine D'Avila-Latourrette "Monastic life": Brother Victor-Antoine D'Avila-Latourrette, *Blessings of the Daily* (Liguori, MO: Liguori/Triumph, 2002) 129; "grows in silence": Latourrette, *Blessings of the Daily*, 80.

Martin Luther All quotations from Martin Luther, *A Simple Way to Pray*, 1535.

Symeon the New Theologian "Even were we": C. J. Decatanzaro, *Symeon the New Theologian: The Discourses* (Mahwah, NJ: Paulist Press, 1980), 91.

Dominic de Guzman "A man who governs": widely attributed to St. Dominic de Guzman; "Do not let": Thomas à Kempis, *The Imitation of Christ: Selections Annotated and Explained* (Woodstock, VT: SkyLight Paths, 2012), 19.

Mother Teresa "Do not look": Franca Zambonini, *Teresa of Calcutta: A Pencil in God's Hand* (New York: Alba House, 1993), 75; "What matters": Zambonini, *Teresa of Calcutta*, xi.

Meister Eckhart "To let go": Amos Smith, *Be Still and Listen: Experience the Presence of God in Your Life* (Brewster, MA: Paraclete Press, 2018).

Clare of Assisi "There's nothing": Wendy Murray, *Clare of Assisi: Gentle Warrior* (Brewster, MA: Paraclete Press, 2020).

Corrie ten Boom All quotations are from Corrie ten Boom, with John and Elizabeth Sherrill, *The Hiding Place* (New York: Bantam Books, 1984).

Seraphim of Sarov Quotations are widely attributed to St. Seraphim of Sarov.

Aelred of Rievaulx "Worldly": Aelred of Rievaulx, *Spiritual Friendship*, trans. Mary Eugenia Laker (Kalamazoo, MI: Cistercian Publications, 1977), 54; "My friend must be": Aelred of Rievaulx. *Spiritual Friendship*, 32; Some information from Karen Wright Marsh, *Vintage Saints and Sinners: 25 Christians Who Transformed My Faith* (Downers Grove, IL: InterVarsity Press, 2017), 155–156.

Francis de Sales All quotations are taken from Bernard Bangley's modern interpretation of Francis de Sales's *Introduction to the Devout Life*, titled *Authentic Devotion* (Colorado Springs, CO: Shaw Books, 2002).

John of the Cross "As fire consumes": John of the Cross, *Dark Night of the Soul*, book 2, chapter 6.5.

Abba Antony All quotations from Ward, *The Sayings of the Desert Fathers*, 2.

Athanasius of Alexandria "We were the purpose": St. Athanasius, *On the Incarnation of the Word* 4:3–4.

Gerhard Tersteegen A report: "Stress in America: Gen Z," American Psychological Association, October 2018, http://tinyurl.com/497445mh; all quotations from Gerhard Tersteegen, *The Spiritual Flower Garden: 101 Devotional Poems of Gerhard Tersteegen*, trans. Bill C. Hensel, 2014.

Alcuin of York "The most learned": Jessica Brain, "Alcuin of York," Historic UK, http://tinyurl.com/yfh2d8vj; "read humbly": Kempis, *The Imitation of Christ*, 3.

Augustine of Hippo "Take up and read": Saint Augustine of Hippo, *Confessions* VIII. 12.29; "Restless is our heart": Augustine, *Confessions* I. 1.1; "I no longer": Augustine, *Confessions*, VIII. 12.

Charles de Foucauld "Foucauld's originality": Kate White, "The Hidden life of Charles de Foucauld," *National Catholic Reporter*, November 11, 2005, http://tinyurl.com/y94j5h7f.

Ida B. Wells "There must be": quoted in Lena Taylor, "Lessons Learned: Ida B. Wells and Nelson Mandela," Madison365, July 25, 2017, http://tinyurl.com/ezv6bk58; "I do note fear": quoted in Linda O. McMurray, *To Keep the Waters Troubled: The Life of Ida B. Wells* (Oxford: Oxford University Press, 1999).

François Fénelon "All wars are": François Fénelon, *Dialogues of the Dead*, 1692–95; "Each individual": François Fénelon, "Socrate et Alcibiade", *Dialogue des Morts*, 1718; "Our devotion": François Fénelon, *The Complete Fenelon*, trans. and ed. Robert J. Edmonson CJ and Hal M. Helms (Brewster, MA: Paraclete Press, 2008).

Albrecht Dürer "Our experience": Juliet Benner, *Contemplative Vision: A Guide to Christian Art and Prayer* (Downers Grove, IL: InterVarsity Press, 2011); "participate with the artist": Benner, *Contemplative Vision*.

Frederick Buechner "The place God": Frederick Buechner, *Wishful Thinking: A Seeker's ABC* (San Francisco: HarperOne, 1993), 119.

George Washington Carver "I love to think": George Washington Carver, letter to Hubert W. Pelt, February 24, 1930; "Get up": Joshua Abraham Heschel, *God in Search of Man: A Philosophy of Judaism* (New York: Farrar, Straus and Giroux, 1976); "I was practically": William J. Federer, *George Washington Carver: His Life and Faith in His Own Words* (St. Louis: Amerisearch, 2002); "You must learn": Dennis Abrams, *George Washington Carver: Scientist and Educator* (New York: Chelsea House Publications, 2008), 16.

Thea Bowman "We don't want": Bishop Edward K. Braxton, "I'm Going Home Like a Shooting Star! The Remarkable Sister Thea Bowman, F.S.P.A.," Sister Thea Bowman Catholic School, http://tinyurl.com/mrr9teke.

John Baillie "Eternal Father": John Baillie, *A Diary of Private Prayer*, trans. and rev. Susanna Wright (New York: Simon & Schuster, 1949; 1977), 3; "May my love": Baillie, *A Diary of Private Prayer*, 125.

Hodegetria "A window into": Linette Martin, *Sacred Doorways: A Beginner's Guide to Icons* (Brewster, MA: Paraclete Press, 2002).

Christ Pantocrator "Christ was the visible": Alfredo Tradigo, *Icons and Saints of the Eastern Orthodox Church* (Los Angeles: J. Paul Getty Museum, 2006), 242; "The Lord bless": Num 6:24–26.

Index of Mystics and Saints